I Didn't Know That!

Taking care of your HOME, your CAR, and your CAREER

CRE▲TIVE
HOMEOWNER®

I Didn't Know That!

Taking care of your HOME, your CAR, and your CAREER

Patrick O' Keefe

Illustrations by Tad Herr

CREATIVE HOMEOWNER®, Upper Saddle River, New Jersey

I DIDN'T KNOW THAT!

SENIOR EDITOR	Kathie Robitz
SENIOR GRAPHIC DESIGNER	Glee Barre
JUNIOR EDITOR	Angela Hanson
PHOTO COORDINATOR	Mary Dolan
DIGITAL IMAGING SPECIALIST	Frank Dyer
INDEXER	Schroeder Indexing Services
COVER DESIGN	Kathryn Wityk
FRONT & BACK COVER PHOTOGRAPHY	(front, left) Tony Giammarino; all others Dreamstime.com
BACK COVER ILLUSTRATIONS	Tad Herr

CREATIVE HOMEOWNER

VICE PRESIDENT AND PUBLISHER	Timothy O. Bakke
ART DIRECTOR	David Geer
MANAGING EDITOR	Fran J. Donegan
PRODUCTION COORDINATOR	Sara M. Markowitz

Manufactured in the United States of America

Current Printing (last digit)
10 9 8 7 6 5 4 3 2 1

I Didn't Know That, First Edition
Library of Congress Control Number: 2009940224
ISBN-10: 1-58011-488-1
ISBN-13: 978-1-58011-488-2

CREATIVE HOMEOWNER®
A Division of Federal Marketing Corp.
24 Park Way
Upper Saddle River, NJ 07458
www.creativehomeowner.com

Safety

Although the methods in this book have been reviewed for safety, it is not possible to overstate the importance of using the safest methods you can. What follows are reminders—some do's and don'ts of work safety—to use along with your common sense.

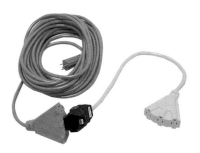

- Always use caution, care, and good judgment when following the procedures described in this book.
- Always be sure that the electrical setup is safe, that no circuit is overloaded, and that all power tools and outlets are properly grounded. Do not use power tools in wet locations.
- Always read container labels on paints, solvents, and other products; provide ventilation; and observe all other warnings.
- Always read the manufacturer's instructions for using a tool, especially the warnings.
- Use hold-downs and push sticks whenever possible when working on a table saw. Avoid working short pieces if you can.
- Always remove the key from any drill chuck (portable or press) before starting the drill.
- Always pay deliberate attention to how a tool works so that you can avoid being injured.
- Always know the limitations of your tools. Do not try to force them to do what they were not designed to do.
- Always make sure that any adjustment is locked before proceeding. For example, always check the rip fence on a table saw or the bevel adjustment on a portable saw before starting to work.
- Always clamp small pieces to a bench or other work surface when using a power tool.
- Always wear the appropriate rubber gloves or work gloves when handling chemicals, moving or stacking lumber, working with concrete, or doing heavy construction.
- Always wear a disposable face mask when you create dust by sawing or sanding. Use a special filtering respirator when working with toxic substances and solvents.
- Always wear eye protection, especially when using power tools or striking metal on metal or concrete; a chip can fly off, for example, when chiseling concrete.
- Never work while wearing loose clothing, open cuffs, or jewelry; tie back long hair.

- Always be aware that there is seldom enough time for your body's reflexes to save you from injury from a power tool in a dangerous situation; everything happens too fast. Be alert!
- Always keep your hands away from the business ends of blades, cutters, and bits.
- Always hold a circular saw firmly, usually with both hands.
- Always use a drill with an auxiliary handle to control the torque when using large-size bits.
- Always check your local building codes when planning new construction. The codes are intended to protect public safety and should be observed to the letter.
- Never work with power tools when you are tired or when under the influence of alcohol or drugs.
- Never cut tiny pieces of wood or pipe using a power saw. When you need a small piece, saw it from a securely clamped longer piece.
- Never change a saw blade or a drill or router bit unless the power cord is unplugged. Do not depend on the switch being off. You might accidentally hit it.
- Never work in insufficient lighting.
- Never work with dull tools. Have them sharpened, or learn how to sharpen them yourself.
- Never use a power tool on a workpiece—large or small—that is not firmly supported.
- Never saw a workpiece that spans a large distance between horses without close support on each side of the cut; the piece can bend, closing on and jamming the blade, causing saw kickback.
- When sawing, never support a workpiece from underneath with your leg or other part of your body.
- Never carry sharp or pointed tools, such as utility knives, awls, or chisels, in your pocket. If you want to carry any of these tools, use a special-purpose tool belt that has leather pockets and holders.

CONTENTS

DEDICATION

To my father-in-law, Russ, thank you! You've taught me a great deal, and more than you realize. To my wife, Donna, my children, Jennifer, Katie, and Steven, my sons-in-law, Rome and Mark, thanks. You've all been extremely supportive, helping me pull this together. Here it is, kids; take Grandpa and me along with you.

To my father and my brother, both named Joe, who served their country in time of need. Both were police officers and dads, and they left this earth way too early.

INTRODUCTION

You've heard the expression, "Jack of all trades, master of none?" If it fits your description, this book is for you. *I Didn't Know That* offers basic guidance to help young men and women—or anyone else who needs it—become self-reliant and confident about everyday matters that are important. For example, you'll learn the smart way to look for an apartment or shop for a house; what to do if the lights go out; how to unclog a drain; how to patch a hole in a wall; and other household issues.

You'll also get some good information about buying versus leasing a car, and how to get the best deal, followed up by easy car repairs and maintenance and wise advice for handling yourself safely on the road.

Finally, *I Didn't Know That* explains how to handle yourself professionally in the job market and how to make the most of your money.

TAD HERR

ABOUT YOUR

part I

HOME

YOUR FIRST PLACE

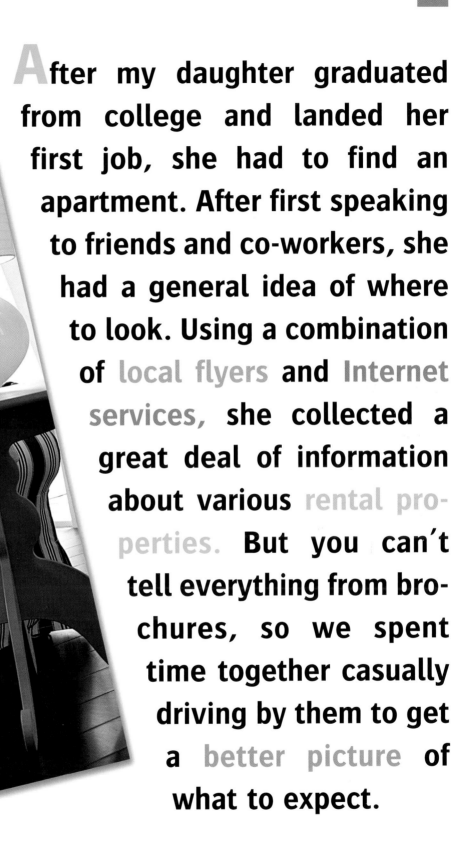

After my daughter graduated from college and landed her first job, she had to find an apartment. After first speaking to friends and co-workers, she had a general idea of where to look. Using a combination of local flyers and Internet services, she collected a great deal of information about various rental properties. But you can't tell everything from brochures, so we spent time together casually driving by them to get a better picture of what to expect.

APARTMENT HUNTING CHECKLIST

INFORMATION
Apartment Name
Address
# of Units
Contact
Phone
Hours to view

DESCRIPTION OF UNIT
Square feet
Level/floor
Bedrooms
Fireplace
Air conditioning
Storage
Appliances
   Refrigerator
   Dishwasher
   Washer/dryer
     or hook-up
   Microwave
   Garbage disposer
Security
Front door viewer
Smoke detectors
Carbon monoxide
   detector
Guest policy
Pet policy
Wall hangings (holes)
Wall color
Public laundry
Ceiling fans
Front door faces
   which way?
Rear view
Parking
Deck/porch
Outdoor grill
Club house
Gym
Pool

Early move-in charge
Renter's insurance
   requirement
On-site landlord
   or super

ITEMIZED COSTS
Monthly rent
Security deposit
Application fee
Phone
Cable TV
Internet
Utilities
   Water
   Electric
   Heat
   Fuel
   Sewage
   Trash haul
   Parking

DISCOUNTS & REBATES
Signing rebate
Internet coupon
Referral

The exterior condition of a building is one indicator of how much the landlord cares about maintenance and repairs.

Choosing an Apartment

from the outside, "Dad" was looking at the age, style, and condition of the cars in the parking lot of each apartment building or complex that may daughter and I looked at, trying to draw a profile of their owners and how they might be as neighbors. Let's face it, when you see hot rods or broken-down pickup trucks, you probably won't be saying, "Good morning, Dr. Williams" to your neighbor!

I also made careful notes about the upkeep of the grounds and the building. A dilapidated porch, patched-up roof, or ripped-off gutters are a sign that the landlord doesn't care—so don't expect much from him or her. If the apartment complex allows dogs, that might be great for your Fluffy, but you should expect to put up with the noise and "presents" from the neighbors' dogs.

You don't want a place too close to a highway or an airport, one that doesn't look well kept, or one where you think safety might be an issue, either. If the washer and dryer are not inside the apartment, consider the security of the laundry area, especially if you do your laundry at night.

When we narrowed down the search to five properties, my daughter made appointments to view each one. She also developed her own "Apartment-Hunting Checklist," opposite, which was useful in making sure all the appropriate questions were asked. It also helped her to keep track of the costs and features of each apartment. It's a good reference for anyone who is looking for an apartment.

i didn't know that...

LEASE DON'TS
You shouldn't sign any lease that:

◀ holds you responsible for legal fees incurred by the landlord for taking legal action against you.

◀ holds the landlord harmless against any personal liability claims for their negligence.

◀ allows the landlord to take your property in the case of a dispute.

The Lease

a lease is a contract you make with the owner of a rental property that spells out the conditions that allow you to live there. The landlord usually decides the terms, which will include the amount of the security deposit. (See "What's a Security Deposit?," opposite.)

Your lease will state how much rent you will pay and when it is due. It may also contain rules and regulations, such as whether or not you are permitted to have a pet in the apartment or paint the walls any color other than white or beige. By signing it, you are legally bound to pay for the entire period of the lease, which is typically one year, but it could be longer or simply month-to-month. A landlord may be able to hold you responsible for the full amount of the term of the lease if you leave before that time, but usually only after demonstrating an inability to rent the property after you move out. You should inquire about your recourse should you break your lease— not that you plan on doing so. Expect to lose at least your security deposit and perhaps another month's rent.

At the expiration of your lease, a portion of your security deposit may be used to recoup any damage or excessive cleaning that might be required to rent the property to someone else—but there must be a clear and specific explanation as to why and how much. You should not be responsible for items that fall under "the ordinary wear and tear in the normal course of habitation," unless it's in the lease and you agreed to it. Different states have different laws, but once a lease has expired, a landlord has a specified amount of time in which to return your security deposit. Make sure you notify your landlord of your forwarding address by registered mail.

WHAT'S A SECURITY DEPOSIT?

A security deposit is an advance of at least one month's rent that is refunded at the end of the lease, provided that you have not violated any of the terms of the contract, including those pertaining to the condition of the property. Before signing, inspect the apartment thoroughly, including all appliances, windows, doors, carpeting, and so forth, making careful notes about its condition. Take pictures, and make sure the landlord has noted and initialed your notes, as well.

break the lease; lose the deposit

what would you do?

HANDLING DISAGREEMENTS

You find yourself in an adversarial relationship with your landlord. Would you

◀ a. leave a message on his answering machine demanding immediate attention

◀ b. stop paying your rent

◀ c. give your landlord notice of the situation via registered mail; then allow a reasonable amount of time to correct it?

During the term of the lease, if you want problems addressed, remember three things: notice, registered mail, and reasonable time. If the landlord fails to address your concerns, assuming they are reasonable and covered by your lease, a court of law might be your only alternative. The court will look at whether the landlord knew of and was given a fair opportunity to address the problem. Because the landlord might be held responsible for your court costs, registered mail will most likely get his attention. So the answer above is "c."

Conversely, if you receive a certified letter from your landlord, pay close attention. If you fail to address and reply to the letter by certified mail, you could be setting yourself up for a court action in which you could be held responsible for your landlord's court costs.

Renting a Moving Van

if you plan to save money by renting a small truck or van and move yourself, the rental company may quote a very low daily rental rate, but keep in mind that that's not the key consideration.

The rate per mile is what's really important. You need to know and compare how much each rental company will charge you per mile of travel. That's how they really make their money.

The second thing to remember is that reservations aren't worth much, particularly in a college town. Make yours early, and verify it several times prior to the pickup date, getting the names of everyone with whom you have spoken. On the day of the event, call again first thing in the morning or, better yet, be at the doorstep when the rental company opens.

Contact your car-insurance agent to ask whether your policy covers rental vehicles. Many policies do, which means that you can waive the rental company's high-price optional insurance fees. Bring a copy of your policy with you on the day of the rental. It's also a good idea to take pictures of any pre-existing scratches or damages on the vehicle and note them on the rental agreement.

A little extra time and consideration given to finding and moving into a new apartment will make the experience less stressful.

Check your rental agreement before formally taking action against your landlord.

BUYING A HOUSE

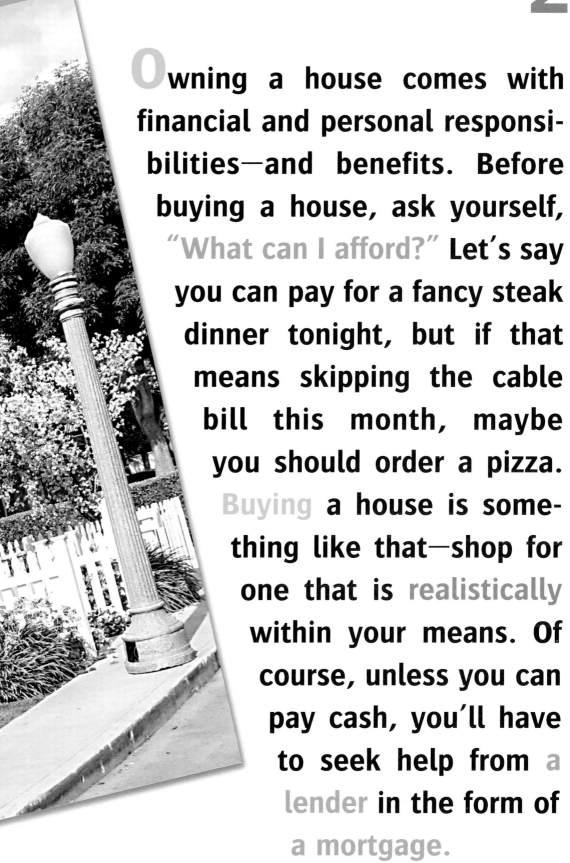

Owning a house comes with financial and personal responsibilities—and benefits. Before buying a house, ask yourself, "What can I afford?" Let's say you can pay for a fancy steak dinner tonight, but if that means skipping the cable bill this month, maybe you should order a pizza. Buying a house is something like that—shop for one that is realistically within your means. Of course, unless you can pay cash, you'll have to seek help from a lender in the form of a mortgage.

A Mortgage?
What Exactly Is That?

a mortgage is your legal promise to pay back a loan secured by the property you are buying. Among the most common types of mortgages are 30-, 20-, or 15-year fixed-rate loans, where the interest rate remains the same throughout the life of the loan. If you plan on selling the house within a few years, a short-term adjustable-rate mortgage (ARM) may be for you. An ARM typically carries a lower interest rate than a fixed-rate mortgage. However, that rate may go up or down over the life of the loan. The loan agreement will spell out when the rate changes will occur.

After the interest is figured into the loan, plan on paying back about double your principal, which is the amount you are borrowing, over the life of the mortgage. In the early years of a fixed-rate mortgage loan, almost all of your monthly mortgage payment goes toward paying off the loan's interest, and almost nothing goes toward reducing the principal.

Your lender or financial advisor can explain the many types of mortgages in more detail and help you decide which one is right for you. You can also become prequalified for a mortgage loan by a lender. This is a simple process of analyzing your income and expenses to determine your mortgage affordability level. In fact, realtors—and many sellers—prefer to deal with prequalified buyers because they have demonstrated that they are financially capable.

If you want to get a jump-start on the prequalification process, spend an afternoon making a list of your weekly and monthly expenditures, and include any new ones you can anticipate as a homeowner—property taxes, for example. You may have to estimate where necessary, or call friends or relatives for their experiences with these expenses. This will give you some idea of what you should spend and the loan payment you can afford. Then look for a mortgage estimator on the Internet (posted on the Web sites of most lending institutions) to find out what your monthly payment will be, depending on how much you borrow and the interest rate. But remember that this does not account for property taxes or insurance, which could add several hundred dollars per month to your payment.

i didn't know that...

WHERE TO GET A LOAN
Although most buyers go to a bank for a mortgage loan, other institutions, such as credit unions, mortgage brokers, and mortgage companies, also make loans available. Shop around for the best deal, interest rate, closing cost, and points. (For closing costs and points, see page 26.)

House Shopping

don't waste time looking on your own. Find a realtor to represent you, but make sure that no buyer fees will be involved. By law, the seller's realtor will always act in the best interest of the seller—not you. But if a realtor is helping you find a house, that person is working as your agent and by law must act in your best interest—not the seller's.

Sales commissions are negotiated by the seller and then split between the seller's and buyer's brokers. The more you spend, the more realtors make, so their interests are best served showing you homes at the higher end of your price range. Although the seller pays the broker fees, the money comes from you in the end. For each additional $1,000 you pay the seller, approximately $60 goes to the realtors.

WHAT TO EXPECT FROM A HOUSE INSPECTION

The following is a summary of items a professional inspector should examine and assess for you in writing.

- foundation and structural problems
- signs of basement flooding
- damaged siding
- wood rot and obvious insect damage
- drainage issues
- sagging roofs and roof condition
- attic and attic insulation
- plumbing fixtures
- water heaters
- heating, ventilation, and air-conditioning systems
- oil tank

- fireplace and chimney flues
- electrical system
- smoke and carbon monoxide detectors
- a full test of all appliances included in the sale
- garage door and garage-door opener
- windows, skylights, doors, and locks

If the house has a basement or a crawl space, have the radon level checked and check for wood-eating insect infestation. This may cost you a few extra dollars, but it is well worth it.

When you're working with a realtor, ask him or her for a list of properties from the Multiple Listing Service (MLS) that are within your price range—and not just the ones that the brokerage firm represents. If the realtor is unwilling to do this, find another one.

After searching the MLS, drive by what seems to be available in your desired area and price range on your own. Then schedule an appointment to view only those properties that appeal to you.

If you have young children, look for swing sets, jungle gyms, and school bus stops. Check out the neighborhood again on a weekend afternoon and evening to see what goes on in that area when it's not a school day or work night. Take a walk. Look for barking dogs, poorly kept nearby properties, or loud music. These are all signs that your neighbors could make you miserable. Stop by the local county or city police department, and ask about crime statistics in the area; then search the Internet for a list and location of local child offenders.

Never buy a home in an area where housing rentals are increasing or nearby property values are declining. Let someone else who better understands the real estate market take the risk.

what would you do?

HOUSE INSPECTION

A house inspection will cost several hundred dollars or more, depending on the size of the home and its location. With the down payment and other related fees, money will be tight. Would you

a. buy a newer home; assume everything is in tiptop shape; and leave it at that

b. rely on the seller's home inspection report

c. hire an independent house inspector at your own expense?

Any offer you make on a house should be contingent on a home inspection. You, not the seller, should hire the inspection firm. Look for one with a professional affiliation, such as the American Society of Home Inspectors (ASHI). Problems in need of correction allow you to negotiate a lower price—or to stipulate that the problems must be corrected prior to your taking possession of the house. The correct answer is "c."

For informat...
a new loan, please call:...

n this portion of the statement, detach and mail to address listed for Inquiries on the reverse side.

Details of Amount Due/Paid

Principal and Interest	$1,579.78
Subsidy/Buydown	$0.00
Escrow	$472.87
Amount Past Due	$0.00
Outstanding Late Charges	$0.00
Other	$0.00
Total Amount Due	$2,052.65
Account Due Date	December 01, 2009

Closing Costs

On the day that you close on your house—when all the papers have been signed, the buyer has been paid, the deed is transferred to your name, and you receive the keys—you will have to write a check for closing costs. Lenders will charge money for items such as title insurance, property appraisal, points, loan origination fees, document preparation fees, credit reports, lender's inspection fees, flood certification, and tax services, which are all included in closing costs. But they could also include prorated water, electric, property-tax bills or homeowner's association dues that the previous owner paid. Potential lenders will provide an estimate of these costs so that you can make comparisons at the beginning of the loan-application process.

Points. A point is a charge by the lender of 1 percent of the amount you borrow. But each point you pay may give you a lower interest rate. Ask the lender whether there is a charge for a yield-spread premium, in which closing costs are covered by a slight increase in the interest rate. That increase could add up to a great deal of money over time.

PERSONAL MORTGAGE INSURANCE (PMI)

When applying for a mortgage, a lender generally prefers that you, the borrower, put down some of your own money as equity. Equity is the value of the home, less the principal amount you owe on it. The larger the down payment, the more likely you will be considered a good credit risk.

If you apply for a mortgage putting down less than 20 percent equity, the lender might require Personal Mortgage Insurance (PMI), which protects the lender in the event you default on the loan. Once your equity in the home reaches 20 percent of its fair market value, you can request cancellation of the PMI, saving you hundreds of dollars per year. Once your equity reaches 22 percent, the PMI should automatically cancel.

i didn't know that...

PAY IT FORWARD?

You can make extra payments on your mortgage loan and have them applied directly toward reducing the principal. The faster you reduce the principal, the less interest you pay the bank, and the sooner you pay back the loan. However, the interest on your loan is tax deductible, so you may want to think carefully about doing this. Ask your accountant how to proceed to get the best benefit for your situation.

SELLING YOUR HOUSE

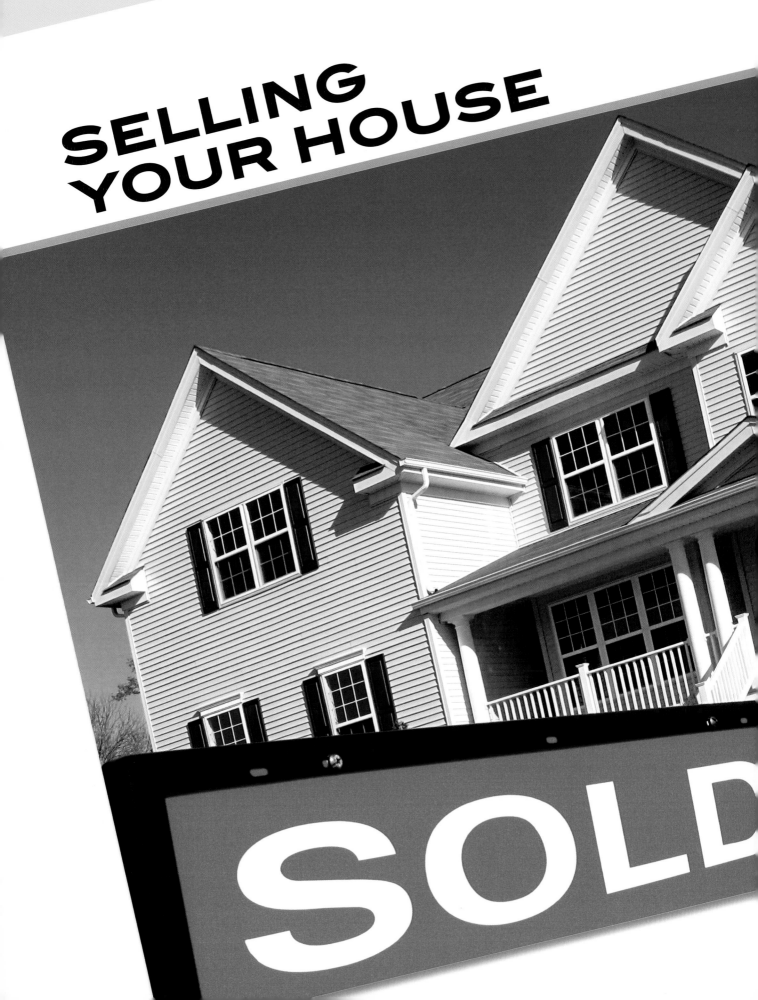

SOLD

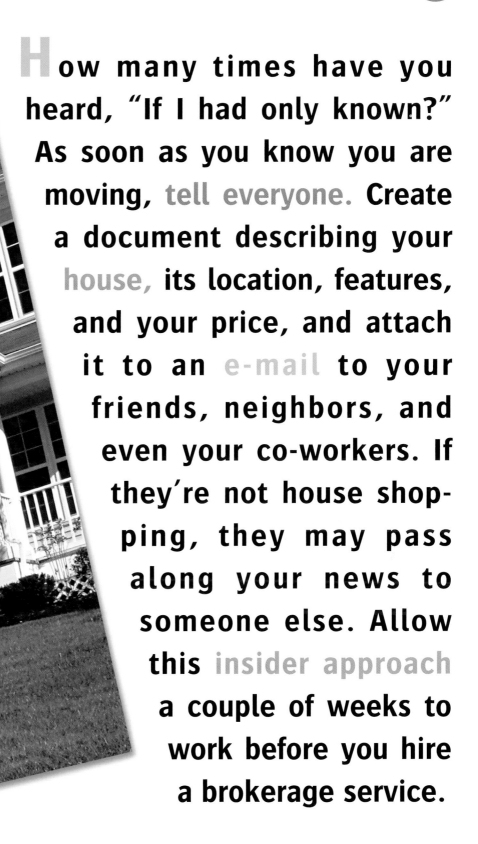

How many times have you heard, "If I had only known?" As soon as you know you are moving, tell everyone. Create a document describing your house, its location, features, and your price, and attach it to an e-mail to your friends, neighbors, and even your co-workers. If they're not house shopping, they may pass along your news to someone else. Allow this insider approach a couple of weeks to work before you hire a brokerage service.

Going Broker—Again!

i f you can sell your home without a broker, you could save 5 to 7 percent of your sale price. That's $5,000 to $7,000 on a $100,000 house and $10,000 to $14,000 if you sell it for $200,000. Keep in mind, not having a broker doesn't mean you shouldn't hire a lawyer to provide you with legal representation during the purchase and sale transaction.

If you don't know what your house is worth, perhaps a new neighbor could offer you some insight regarding the current market price in your area. You can also look at nearby homes for sale and obtain sales brochures, check the Web sites of realtors in your area, and scan the real-estate section of the local newspaper. You might also check other online sources, such as www.zillow.com, which provides free real-estate information, including local home prices, values, and recent sales in your area.

The real estate market remains dominated by brokers who have capitalized on the Multiple Listing Service (MLS). This is a database developed by realtors for realtors that lists what properties are on the market in an area. It will also include the asking price and general information, such as the size of the lot and number of rooms. Because access to the MLS is open to all licensed realtors and not just your broker, it expands the pool of potential buyers. If a realtor other than your own makes the sale, he or she will receive a portion of the commission. For now, the only way to have your house included in the MLS is through a licensed real-estate agent. If you don't contract with a broker, you can't get access.

i didn't know that...

PAY WHAT?

The sales commission is a negotiated percentage of the house selling price and is split between the buyer's and seller's brokers. Big-name real-estate firms are probably not as flexible on the percentage as a smaller, more-aggressive local broker may be.

THE RIGHT REALTOR FOR YOU

Relators certainly easy to find. Make a few calls, and arrange a few interviews. Check with neighbors or friends who might be able to recommend someone. Without obligation, prospective realtors are willing to come to your house, look around, and informally discuss your prospects and what they can do to help sell your house. They'll also tell you what commission they charge. Never chose a realtor simply because he or she has suggested the highest sale price for your house. You should carefully consider the length of time in days or months the broker has to sell your home. Make sure the selling price seems reasonable—in line with comparable homes in your area—and the length of time the broker has to sell your house is no more than 90 days.

REAL ESTATE CONTRACT

This real estate contract becomes valid when signed and dated by all pa document becomes a legally binding legal instrument unless cancele days from signing by either party. You may choose to consult an attor stand the terms of this contract. agrees to sell and convey title to Purchaser and Purchaser agr scribed below.

If your house is still on the market after several months, ask your realtor for any feedback he or she has got from people who have looked at your house. This might help identify something about it that turns off buyers; something that you could easily correct. At this point, you may also have to reduce the asking price and, perhaps, find a different realtor. Now you're right back where you started—but with a home that has grown a bit stale having been already scouted and seen by the pool of potential buyers.

Ready the House for Sale

giving a buyer the opportunity to point out needed repairs will only result in a lower offer. So it's wise to hire a home inspector and repair the items listed in the report before you put the house on the market. A few dollars invested this way can result in a financial gain at sale time. Talk to your realtor, who can advise you about what improvements are worth doing and which ones are not. Ask for simple suggestions that can make your house show better, too.

Remember: clutter is bad. Having less stuff around makes rooms seem larger—and larger is good. An organized home presents well, but buyers are trying to imagine how their things will fit in it. So reduce the number of wall hangings, heavy window treatments, and stuff that you keep on the countertops and tables—even if they are neatly arranged. Remove extra furniture, and store it or give it way.

Where possible, repaint walls with a brighter neutral color. Check the light fixtures and all the lightbulbs, and keep them on when your home is being shown. Open the curtains, and make sure the windows sparkle. All kitchen and bathroom appliances and fixtures should be clean and shining, too.

Have the rugs professionally cleaned, and if your home has hardwood floors, show them; don't cover them. Flowers in the hallway or on the kitchen table are a nice touch. I've heard conflicting stories about using scented candles; scents can trigger all the right—or wrong—associations. If you have a pet, there are special cleaning products that you can use to dissipate or reduce those odors.

PLAY UP THE NEIGHBORHOOD

Take a moment to write out all the great things about the community, especially your neighborhood. List those things you'd like to know if you were shopping for a home—distance to stores, churches, schools, and the things going on in the community are good examples. Make it a nonprofessional, one-page list of all the attributes. Write at the top of the page, "Things about Our Neighborhood." Let your agent know what you are doing, and then place the list in plain view on the kitchen table where prospective buyers will clearly see it when they're touring your house.

CALL ATTENTION

Does your home have a number of updates, such as a new water heater, furnace, appliances, and so forth? If so, make a list of "New Features," and leave it on the kitchen table or post little notes on each one throughout the house. For example, write "New Furnace 2006."

what would  you do?

CURB APPEAL

You live in a neighborhood where most of the houses look the same—and besides yours, there is another one for sale on your block. You've got to find a way to draw attention to your home. Would you

◀ a. mow the lawn, and clean the walks and driveway

◀ b. trim the hedges, and plant a few colorful flowers

◀ c. create an interesting focal point in front of the house, such as a water fountain or an arbor

◀ d. all of the above?

Hopefully, you answered "d." Curb appeal means everything. Keep the exterior of the house neat and updated. Small projects can make a big difference in both the appearance of your house and how much money you may be offered for it. It doesn't cost a lot to paint the front door and install new hardware and house numbers. If you have a few extra dollars, replace old-fashioned light fixtures. And don't forget to buy a new welcome mat.

TOOLS FOR HOME MAINTENANCE

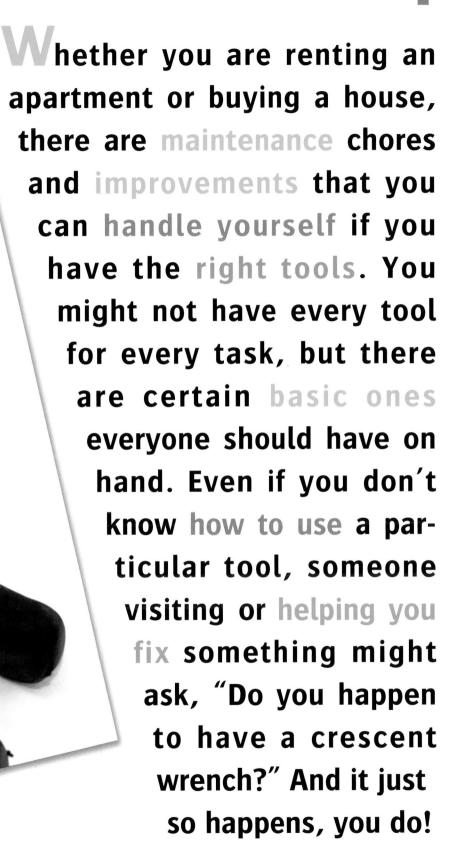

Whether you are renting an apartment or buying a house, there are maintenance chores and improvements that you can handle yourself if you have the right tools. You might not have every tool for every task, but there are certain basic ones everyone should have on hand. Even if you don't know how to use a particular tool, someone visiting or helping you fix something might ask, "Do you happen to have a crescent wrench?" And it just so happens, you do!

Tool Time

i n chapters 4 through 11, you'll learn how to make some basic home improvements and repairs. But in the meantime, if you don't already have a basic tool kit, head to your local hardware store or home-improvement center. Then hand the salesman the list of tools provided in "A Basic Home Tool Kit" shown at right. Pricey? A little. Essential? Absolutely!

i didn't know that...

THE TURN OF THE SCREW

If you're having trouble driving a screw into a hard surface or a thick piece of wood, apply soap to the threads. Bingo!

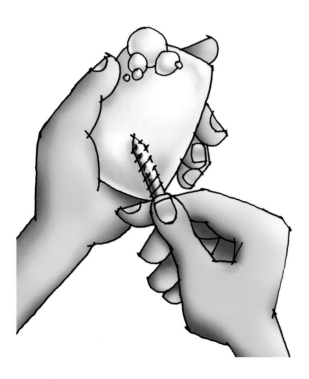

A BASIC HOME TOOL KIT

If you're a total novice to the world of home improvement and maintenance, or you'd rather pay someone to do all of your repairs, go for the basics—just in case. A barebones tool kit should include the following:

◀ Adjustable crescent wrench
◀ Hammer
◀ Electrician's pliers
◀ Needle-nose pliers
◀ Wire-cutter pliers
◀ Cordless drill/screwdriver with bits
◀ Phillips-head screwdrivers (short, plus small, medium, and large)
◀ Flat-blade screwdrivers (short, plus small, medium, and large)
◀ Retractable razor knife
◀ Awl (pronounced "all") for punching holes in drywall and starting screw holes in wood if not predrilling
◀ 15-foot (at least) measuring tape
◀ 2-foot level for picture hanging
◀ Wall-stud finder (a cheap one, usable for hanging pictures)
◀ 5-foot aluminum stepladder
◀ Staple gun

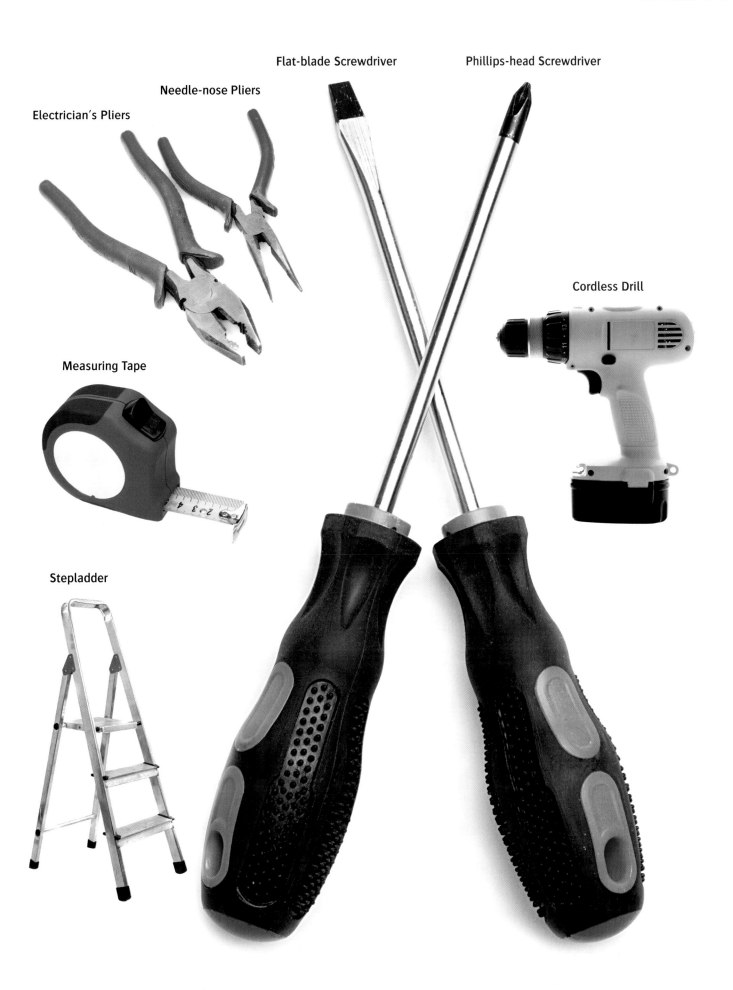

Electrician's Pliers

Needle-nose Pliers

Flat-blade Screwdriver

Phillips-head Screwdriver

Cordless Drill

Measuring Tape

Stepladder

AN ADVANCED HOME TOOL KIT

If you feel ready to be more adventurous and self-sufficient, you'll need more tools. A more-advanced tool kit includes the following:

- Pliers (channel-lock, vise-grip, and wire-stripping)
- Electrical outlet tester
- Set of ¼- or ³⁄₈-inch-drive rachet wrenches and hex-head nut driver
- 12-inch pry bar
- Hacksaw
- Small wood handsaw
- Yardstick
- Eyeglass screwdriver kit
- Set of Allen wrenches (They fit in Allen screws and bolts, with hex-shape recesses; individual ones look like little black hockey sticks.)
- Set of star head (Torx) wrenches
- 10-inch pipe wrench
- Plumb bob
- Soft rubber mallet

what would you do?

HOW TO CHANGE A MINI-LIGHTBULB

The compact, low-voltage recessed light fixtures in your ceiling look great. But you're having trouble removing burned-out bulbs. The fixture is so small that you can't get a grip on the bulb. Would you

- a. call an electrician
- b. use duct tape to remove the bulbs
- c. leave the burned-out bulbs there and never use the lights again?

You could call in an electrician, but you'll pay a lot of money just to remove a few light bulbs. The best answer is "b." This is one of those times when you'll be glad to have duct tape handy, and if you don't, go out to the hardware store and buy it. Cut a piece of tape—the size of which should cover the bulb and leave enough at each end to fold over and create tabs. Apply the tape to the bulb; fold each end over itself. Grip both of the end tabs between your thumb and index finger, which should help you loosen the bulb by turning it counterclockwise.

You can save money with ready-to-assemble furniture—as long as you have the tools.

A HOME SUPPLIES AND APPLIANCES KIT

There are also a number of supplies and small appliances that everyone should have around the house. They include the following:

- Toilet plungers (one for each bathroom)
- Sink plunger
- Drain clog auger
- Flashlights (several)
- Butane lighter
- Dry-chemical fire extinguishers (one per floor and garage)
- Duct tape
- Electrical tape
- Heavy-duty 50-foot extension cord
- Security light and appliance timers (a couple)
- Paper shredder
- Battery-powered radio

WALLS 101

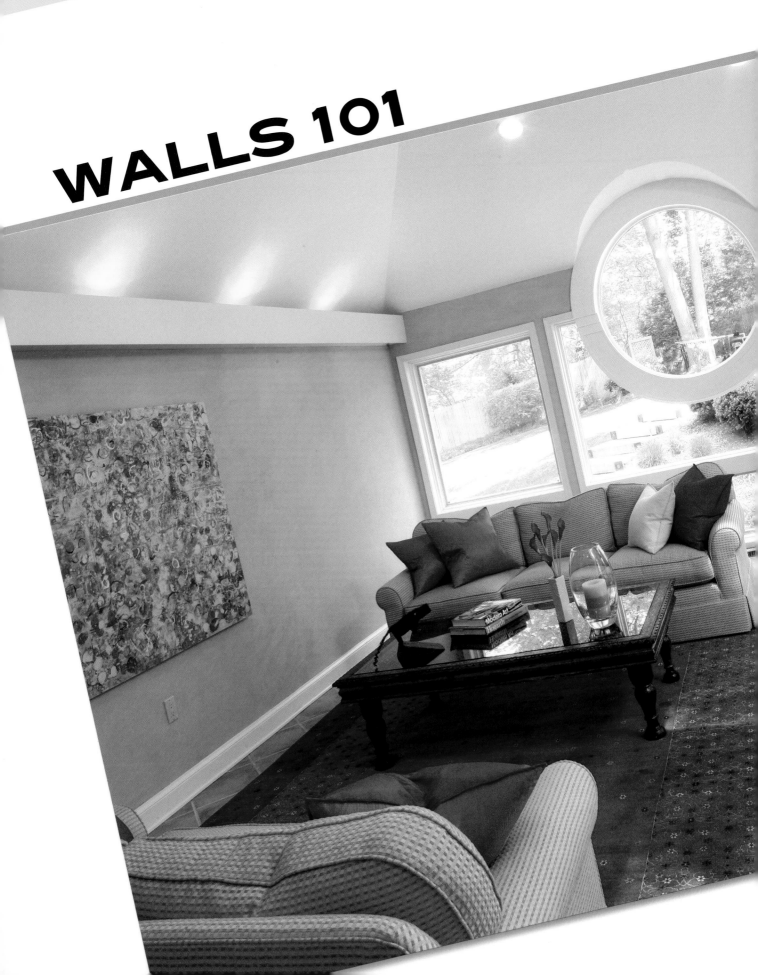

OK, you've made the move into a new home—the furniture has arrived and the boxes have been unpacked. Now what? What are you going to put on all those blank walls? Paint? Wallpaper? A few framed pictures? Projects such as these do not require a great deal of skill or expertise, just a little know-how to make the results of your labor worth the effort that you've made. Besides, doing the job the right way can save time and money.

Painting

One of the first things you'll probably want to do when you move into a new home is paint. It's also one of the easiest and least-expensive ways to freshen up the place and make it your own. For indoor painting, use a latex primer and paint. Latex paint goes on easily, dries fast, and cleans up without a hassle because it is water soluble. You can clean brushes, rollers, drips, and splatters using soap and water right in the kitchen sink. Alkyd (oil-based) paint and primer, another formula, dries to a harder finish. Generally, it's better for outdoor applications, where it stands up longer to the elements, or in high-traffic areas that will take a lot of abuse. This type of paint is more expensive than latex and contains solvents, which make cleaning brushes or splatters more difficult. In addition, you can dispose of it only under very controlled circumstances. (Check the paint-disposal regulations in your area.)

it's a project anyone can handle

BASIC PAINT SUPPLIES

Stock up on the following items before you paint:

◀ Painter's masking tape
◀ Drop cloths
◀ Putty knife
◀ Drywall joint compound
◀ Medium- and fine-grit sandpaper
◀ Sanding block
◀ Paint can opener
◀ Paint scraper
◀ Paint stirrers

◀ Plastic paint can collar (eliminates pouring drips)
◀ 1½ or 2-inch sash brush (soft bristle)
◀ 9-inch and 3-inch rollers and 3-inch brush
◀ Roller pan
◀ Roller extension
◀ Paint pail (or paint cup) and plastic liners
◀ Clear safety glasses

BUYING PAINT

Bring a sample of the color you want to match to your local paint or home-improvement center. Most of these stores are equipped with a computer system that reads colors digitally and provides the correct mixing formula to achieve a match.

It's smart to try a color in a few places around the room, live with it for a few days, and then decide whether it's right for you. You might be surprised how often the color "changes" by time of day once it's on the walls. To be safe, buy just a quart

Let's Get Started

first, determine whether the ceiling must be painted. Sometimes just taking a broom to it to remove cobwebs and dust is all you need to do. If you decide to paint the ceiling, do it before you tackle the walls. But before you start, make sure you have placed drop cloths over the entire floor surface and all of the furniture. No matter how neat you are, there will always be drips and splatters from the roller or brush.

This is also the time to mask the floorboards and trimwork. Painter's masking tape and an old newspaper torn into thirds cover all of the trim very nicely. Don't use regular masking tape, particularly if the job will take longer than a couple of days. It will dry and leave a glue residue. Paint and hardware stores sell a special painter's masking tape, which comes off neatly and cleanly when the job is done. Also, don't be too fussy about getting the ceiling paint onto the walls, because you will cover this up later with the wall paint. If you're painting the ceiling white over existing white paint, one coat should do it.

i didn't know that...

ECO-FRIENDLY
The type of paint you choose will affect the environment in your home. When you're buying paint, consider purchasing one that is labeled no VOCs (volatile organic compounds), which are toxins that can remain in your home for years.

and test it before you invest in a gallon or more of paint in a color that you might realize you don't like only after it's too late.

In addition, if the paint you're buying comes off the shelf, make sure to have the can machine-shaken before you leave the store.

If you have a can of old paint that you intend to use on the project, bring it back to the paint store, and ask the salesperson to machine-shake it again. If he or she won't do it, flip the old can of paint upside down, and leave it that way for a day or so before using it. This helps to blend the tints by bringing the paint sediment at the bottom of the can to the top.

When you open the can, stir the paint well, making sure to scrape the bottom of the can to loosen any of the remaining "good stuff" (the pigments and tints) that may still be settled there. Do this even with a new can of paint, and repeat it periodically as you work your way across the wall.

By the way, as long as you're buying paint, you shouldn't be charged for the wooden paint sticks.

MINOR **WALL REPAIR**

If you think painting over a damaged wall surface will cover the blemishes, you're going to be disappointed. Even a nail ripped out from a wall may leave a protruding jagged edge of drywall paper. Minor blemishes are not difficult to repair, and it's worth the effort.

First, dimple the area back into the wall using some form of a small rounded end punch. The rounded end of a small carriage bolt works great. You don't have to hit it hard, just enough to create a slight inward depression back into the drywall. Then invest the time to fill in this and any other small holes, dents, scratches, or minor blemishes with Spackle, or drywall joint compound. Sand and prime the areas before painting over them.

1 Using a putty knife, fill in any depression with a base coat of drywall joint compound. Let it dry, and add one or more top coats to build up the damaged area.

2 When the patch dries, make the surface smooth using a sanding block and a sheet of fine sandpaper. Now your walls are ready for you to prime and paint. If you don't plan to prime the walls entirely, at least prime the repaired spots. This will seal the patches and prevent dull areas in the finish coat of paint.

Get to Work

Once you prime the walls, paint the trim. Rather than lugging an entire gallon around the room when you're painting the trim, pour some paint into a small, 1-quart pail or plastic container. (To quicken the cleanup later, use disposable plastic liners for both the paint pail and the roller pan.)

Let the trim dry thoroughly before masking it and painting the walls. Before picking up a roller, spend some time to carefully paint as close to the woodwork as possible using a soft-bristle sash brush. If you've protected the trimwork properly, you won't have to worry about splattering the woodwork. Paint the area just below the ceiling line, in the corners, around outlets, around windows and doors, and just above the base trim near the floor using the same type of brush.

Let this work dry for about an hour. Then pick up the roller, and paint the rest of the wall surface. If a second coat is needed, repeat the entire process. Between coats, wrap wet brushes and rollers inside plastic grocery bags. This is a great way to keep them clean and moist until you're ready to apply the next coat of paint. When you're done, use the plastic bag to pull the pad off the roller sleeve. Throw them both away—but keep the roller frame and roller pan.

Don't forget to save some extra paint for touch-ups. Apply a dab to the side and the top of the paint can to use as a color reference. Write on the can where and when you bought the paint, the custom paint formula, and in which room you used it. Trust me; if you don't write it down, you won't remember it.

i didn't know that...

PAINT ROLLERS

Buy a good-quality roller sleeve. They come in a variety of textures: smooth, medium, and coarse. Make sure you have picked out the right one for your paint. Ask the salesperson for help. When in doubt, go with the medium. Don't skimp on cheap rollers, either—or you will spend a lot of time picking fibers off the wall later.

Wallcovering

you may love it or hate it, but whatever you do, don't paint, or for that matter, wallpaper over a paper or fabric wallcovering. Of course, some people do this, but the result is inferior.

Removing wallpaper takes a little elbow grease, but it's not difficult. First, you have to score the paper—and there is an inexpensive tool you can buy for this purpose. Wet the surface using a wallpaper-removal liquid or with a steamer, which you can rent from a local hardware store. Once the paper starts to loosen, grab one corner and pull it down at an angle. For stubborn spots, use a paint scraper to loosen the paper from the wall—but be careful not to damage the surface by applying too much pressure. After you have removed all of the wallpaper, clean the walls using a sponge soaked in water and trisodium phosphate, or TSP, which is another supply you can find in the hardware store or at the home center. Wait about a week until the walls are thoroughly dry before painting. Applying new wallpaper? Then turn the page.

SPOT REPAIRS

You can make spot repairs to damaged wallpaper. Align a patch piece over the pattern; tape it down; and cut through both layers. Then remove the patch and the cut damaged piece from the wall; the patch should fit exactly in the hole.

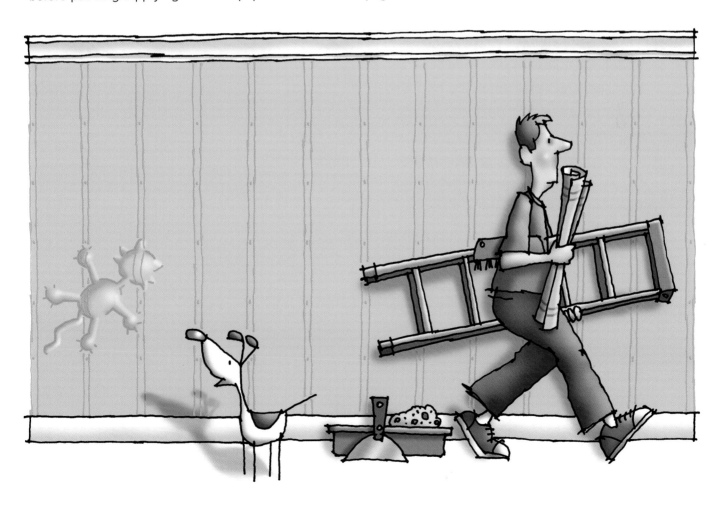

HANGING **WALLPAPER**

This used to be a messy task that required a huge brush and pails of gooey paste. Today's prepasted papers make the project a lot easier. To do the job, you'll need a level, a tray with lukewarm water, a utility knife with lots of sharp blades, a scissors, and a seam roller.

1 Measure out from the starting corner the width of the wallcovering you will be using minus ½ inch. Use a level to mark lines where the first seam will fall.

2 Dunk a strip of the prepasted paper into the tray of water.

3 Fold the soaked roll onto itself (called "booking"), which makes it easier to carry and place the strip on the wall.

4 Unbook the paper, and position it on the wall. Align it at the ceiling and close to your guideline. Then unroll the strip, and press it in place, overlapping the corner by ½ inch.

5 Smooth it with a brush, starting at the top corner and moving down and across.

6 Trim away excess paper at the top and bottom using a utility knife. Then continue with the next strip, and so forth.

7 You can overlap strips to make adjustments and hand-cut through two adjoining strips to match a pattern. (If you're a beginner, stick with a simple random pattern that does not need matching.)

8 Go over all of the seams using the seam roller, and wipe away excess adhesive using a damp sponge.

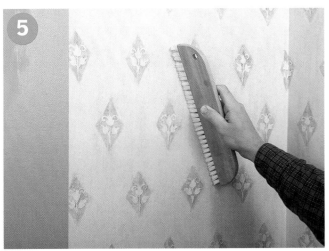

i didn't know that...

TIME OUT

After soaking, prepasted papers should be set aside to absorb the adhesive for the time specified by the manufacturer.

How to Hang Pictures on a Wall

before you mar a wall with nails trying to find the right spot for a picture, make a template. Cut newspaper or brown wrapping paper to the same size as the frame. (This works well for arranging groupings of multiple pictures, but it's just as practical for a positioning a single frame.) Apply the template to the wall using painter's masking tape. Rearrange things until you are satisfied. Use a level to make sure everything is straight, and then mark the spots.

Choosing a Fastener

A nail driven into the wall at 45-degree downward angle might be just fine for small, lightweight items, but not for anything substantial. If you're lucky, the perfect place for your picture will coincide with one of the vertical wooden wall studs (part of the framework of the house behind the drywall). A battery-operated stud finder will help you locate one. If not, you're going to need a wall anchor or a toggle bolt to provide a stable means for hanging heavy pictures on drywall anywhere between the studs.

You can purchase plastic wall anchors and compatible screws as a set. Make a small hole in the wall using a drill bit. The hole should be slightly narrower in diameter than the wall anchor. Using a hammer, tap the anchor into the hole. Some types of wall anchors have threads and have to be screwed into the wall. Do this with a Philips-head screwdriver, or better yet, with a screw gun or a drill with the proper screw-head bit. Drill the anchor into the wall slowly until the fastener is almost flush with the surface. Do not overtighten it. Insert the supplied screw into the wall anchor using a screwdriver, and now you have stable support for hanging most picture frames.

If you're hanging a heavy item, such as a shelf bracket, use a toggle bolt. This fastener works with a slot-head bolt that screws into a folding spring-loaded "wing," which is the toggle. You'll have to attach the bolt to the object you're hanging, and then screw the bolt into the wing and fold the wing in half. Then make a hole in the wall that is the same width as the wing in its folded position. Push the bolt and folded wing into the wall. The wing halves will spring open and anchor, or toggle, the bolt to the wall once you turn it clockwise to tighten its grip.

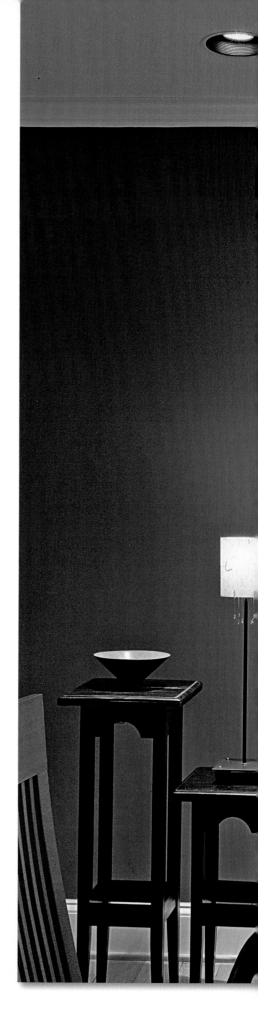

PINPOINT ACCURATE HANGING TIPS

Note the location of the hanging hardware or wire on the back of the picture frame. It's probably an inch or so down from the top. To account for this, place a small strip of masking tape on the top of the frame. Mark the center of the frame on the tape using a pencil. Hold the frame against the wall where you want to hang it and, using the mark on the tape as a guide, make a small mark on the wall.

From there, measure down to account for the hanging hardware or wire, and make a second pencil mark on the wall. Install your nail or hook there. Remove the masking tape from the frame, and hang your picture.

For a long frame, you may have nails or hangers at each end. Follow the directions above, marking the wall at both ends and in the center. Use a level to make sure that the "line" from one end to the other is straight.

ELECTRICAL 101

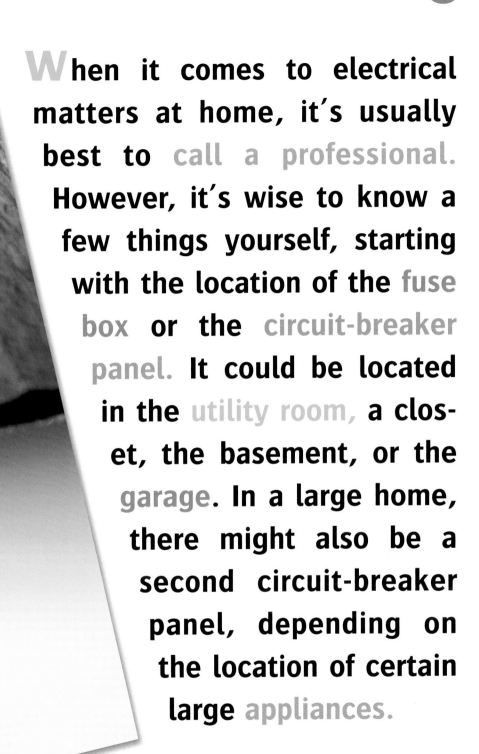

When it comes to electrical matters at home, it's usually best to call a professional. However, it's wise to know a few things yourself, starting with the location of the fuse box or the circuit-breaker panel. It could be located in the utility room, a closet, the basement, or the garage. In a large home, there might also be a second circuit-breaker panel, depending on the location of certain large appliances.

INSIDE YOUR SERVICE PANEL

You should be able to locate your home's service panel in complete darkness using only a flashlight. It's a metal box that is mounted on a wall. Open it, and you should see two columns of circuit-breaker toggle switches (they look something like light switches that have been installed sideways) or circular ceramic or glass fuse plugs that screw into place much like a lightbulb.

You should see the numbers 15, 20, 40, or even 60 on the circuit breakers or fuses. These numbers refer to the amp rating. Ideally, there will be a reference chart on the inside door panel that will indicate which breakers or fuses pertain to the particular zones or appliances.

The main circuit breaker or fuse for all of your home's electricity should be

Circuit breakers

Glass fuses

at the top of the panel. If you trip the switch or pull the fuse, you'd better have a flashlight because everything electrical in the house will shut down. An electrician might do this if he or she is working on a project at your house. Otherwise, leave the "main" alone.

The Service Panel

the service panel is where the electrical supply from your utility company comes into your home after it passes through a meter that receives the electricity through overhead or underground wires. The electricity is divided at the service panel into separate branches, or circuits—for example, the master bedroom may be one circuit, the front porch and entry another, and so forth. High-power-consuming appliances may require their own circuits.

The service panel will contain circuit-breaker switches, or in older homes, circular ceramic or glass fuses, for the different circuits that will have different amperage (amp) ratings. (Electrical current is measured in amperes, or amps.) The rating for each circuit will be marked on the circuit breaker or fuse, usually 15 or 20 amps for most room circuits and 30 to 50 amps for heavy-duty circuits, such as those serving an electric kitchen range, clothes dryer, or water heater. Should an electrical circuit draw more current than the wiring was designed to handle, it will "trip." That means the current will be cut off by the circuit breaker or fuse.

i didn't know that...

PLAY IT SAFE
With older fuse boxes, it's never a good idea to replace a burned-out 15-amp fuse with a 20-amp fuse, or vice versa. A higher-amp-rated fuse will not trip (cut off electricity) if the circuit becomes overloaded, which is a fire hazard. If you believe fuses are blowing out too often, hire an electrician to inspect your fuse box and circuits.

what would you do?

AN OFF AND ON THING

You're in your room, blow-drying your hair; you've got an iron heating; and the TV is on. All of a sudden your blow-dryer stops, and the lights and TV go out. What happened? Your appliances most likely overloaded the electrical circuit, blowing a fuse or tripping a breaker. Would you

a. shut off the appliances that you were using, and reset the breaker or replace the fuse

b. shut off the appliances that you were using, and wait for the power to come back on

c. call your landlord?

The correct answer is "a." If you're renting, you could call the landlord, but it's not necessary unless you don't have access to the service panel. A tripped breaker should be easy to spot. It will be the one that is not quite in the "on" or "off" position. To reset it, simply snap the toggle switch completely to "off"; then snap it completely over to the "on" side. To determine whether a fuse is burned out, look into its center to see whether there is a blackened area. If so, the fuse is burned out and must be replaced. You should keep a supply of 15- and 20-amp fuses nearby and ready if necessary. With dry hands, it is safe to touch and unscrew a fuse, but never stick your finger into an empty fuse socket.

As a safety precaution, make sure that you have a flashlight on hand and that there is enough light to see what you're doing when you have to change a fuse or reset a circuit breaker. Always take extreme care anytime you are working with electricity.

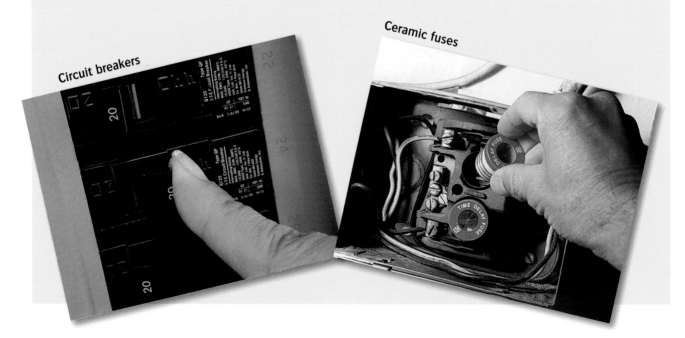

Ceramic fuses

Circuit breakers

Short Circuits

If a breaker fails to hold in position or a fuse continually blows, there could be a constant overload or a short circuit somewhere in the electrical circuit or appliance. If so, make sure you have unplugged all electrical devices on that circuit, and then try resetting the breaker or replace the fuse. If it resets, something you unplugged was the cause of the problem. Carefully examine the plug of each electrical cord for burn marks or frayed wires. If you find either of them, do not use the appliance. Start plugging back in each electrical device one at a time to see which device caused the circuit to blow. One more thing: although it doesn't happen often, a breaker could also go bad and need to be replaced. That would be a job for a professional.

Surge protector

WHAT TO DO IN A POWER OUTAGE

If your home loses all power, first look up and down the street to see whether the street lights or your neighbors' lights are working. If not, all you can do is wait for the power to be restored. This is where a flashlight and a battery-powered radio come in handy.

Your landline phone should still work unless you have cable modem service through the Internet. In that case, use your cell phone. Check with a neighbor and the power company to investigate what's causing the problem.

Shut down your air-conditioning unit during a power outage. (You should have your TV, DVD player, and computers protected by electrical surge suppressors.)

By the way, unless your home's water supply comes from a private well and electric pump, sinks and toilets will continue to operate normally. If your water supply is driven by an electric pump, you can pour bottled water into the toilet tank, and it will flush.

If you believe the power will be out for a while, pull out the cooler, head to the store, and stock up on ice—before everyone else does—particularly if you have medicine that must be kept cold. If the inside temperature of the refrigerator rises and perishable food is at risk, pack the food with the ice into the cooler.

Watch for rising ground water, if you have an electric sump pump in the basement. A battery-powered backup sump pump is a good idea and may save you lots of aggravation in such an emergency.

When the power returns and you're frantically running around resetting all the clocks, don't forget to check the programming on the setback thermostat and water softener.

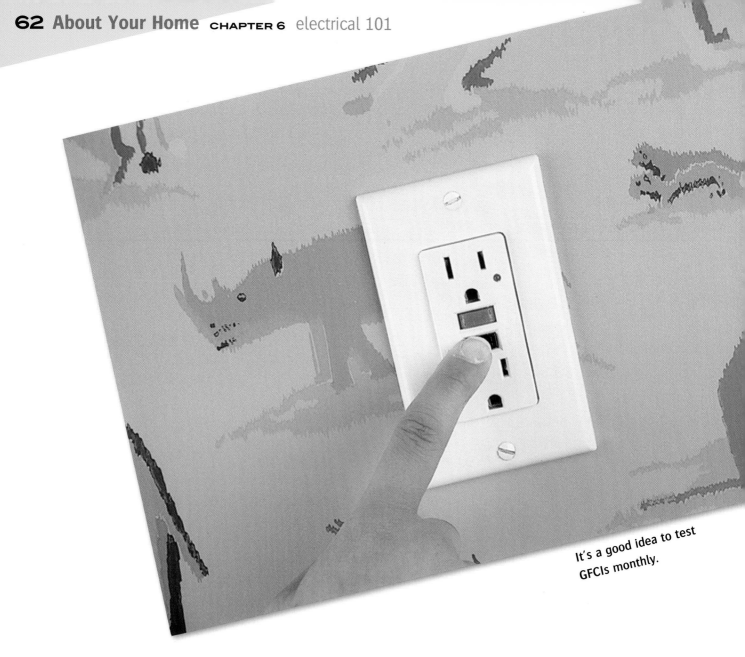

It's a good idea to test GFCIs monthly.

Ground-Fault Circuit Interrupters (GFCIs)

in damp areas around the house or in places that are exposed to water—the bathroom, kitchen, laundry room, garage, basement, and outdoor areas—you may find outlets that look a little different from standard electrical outlets because they are connected to a device called a ground-fault circuit interrupter, or GFCI. You'll notice that in the center of a GFCI-equipped outlet, there are two buttons— one is yellow or black and says "test;" the other is red and says "reset." If you don't have GFCIs in the wet or damp locations in your home, have them installed by an electrician immediately. They are required for new construction by the National Electrical Code.

i didn't know that...

GFCIs are sensitive to a ground fault or electrical line leakage and will immediately shut down the power to that circuit. So if you accidentally drop your electric shaver into a sink full of water, the GFCI will trip and the power will instantly shut off, keeping you safe from electrical shock.

You should test all GFCIs monthly. It only takes a few seconds. Plug your hair dryer or shaver into the outlet, and turn it on. Next, hit the yellow or black test button, which should shut off the appliance. Restore the electrical connection by pushing in the red reset button. If it doesn't restore, call an electrician to replace the device.

DONT GET ZAPPED

If lightning strikes your home, it can send thousands of volts of electricity through the wiring system into an appliance you may be using—and into you. So stay away from all electrical appliances during a lightning storm. Stay off the landline phone, too, and use your cell phone. Surge suppressors aren't much help in this type of situation, either. To fully protect your major electrical components, unplug them.

what would you do?

REMOVING A BROKEN LIGHTBULB

This is certainly not a life skill or a résumé enhancer, but would you know what to do if a lightbulb breaks off and the metal base remains in the socket?

Would you

◄ a. pry it out using a flat-blade screwdriver

◄ b. cut it out using a utility knife

◄ c. jam a potato into the socket and twist?

That's right, it's "c." But first, put on a pair of safety glasses; you will be dealing with fragments of broken glass. Then flip the light switch to the "off" position. If you're unsure whether you've actually turned off the light switch, locate the circuit breaker or fuse that controls the light, and flip the circuit-breaker switch to "off" or unscrew the fuse.

Cut a potato in half, and jam one of the sliced ends into the socket in order to imbed the glass and metal base in the spud. Twist, and voilà!

If a potato isn't handy, you'll need a pair of rubber-gripped, needle-nose pliers, along with your safety glasses. Again, shut off the light.

This isn't as easy as the potato fix, but it works. Looking at the socket as you would the face of a clock, use the needle-nose pliers to grab the top outer edge of the metal base at the 9 o'clock position. If broken glass remnants are visible, don't worry. The thin bulb remnants will easily break apart as you grab the metal base.

While squeezing the pliers tightly with your right hand, use your left hand for leverage to help create a downward pressure, coaxing the metal base toward the 6 o'clock position. Remember, you're not trying to pull the metal base out, but down slightly and to the left to begin the unscrewing process. It might take some wiggling to get it started, but build upon small amounts of progress by repeating the process described. Eventually, it will get easier and the metal base will give way, becoming very loose and cooperative.

NOTE: If you are using compact fluorescent light bulbs (CFLs) in your home, you should know that they contain mercury. When you need to replace a CFL, or if one breaks, dispose of it safely and in accordance with the recommendations from the Environmental Protection Agency (EPA) at www.epa.gov/hg/spills/#fluorescent.

REPLACING A LIGHT SOCKET AND SWITCH

This is a simple repair that can save you the cost of a new lamp. You can buy the parts in any hardware store or home center, and they are inexpensive. You can do the job in four easy steps. Make sure to unplug the lamp before you start.

1 Remove the U-shape harp (which holds the lampshade) by raising the stays, squeezing the arms, and lifting. Squeeze the brass sleeve above the socket base cap, and slip off both the sleeve and the inside insulator (often cardboard).

2 Loosen the terminal screws; disconnect the wires; and remove the old switch.

3 Connect the hot (copper) wires to the new socket. The wires should fit under the terminal screws; if not, re-twist them.

4 Place the insulator and brass shell over the socket. Tighten the setscrew holding the cord in the socket, if there is one, and replace the harp.

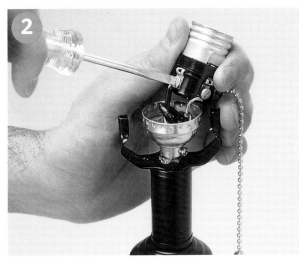

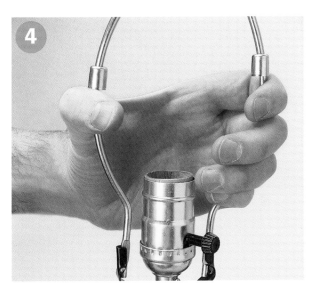

PLUMBING 101

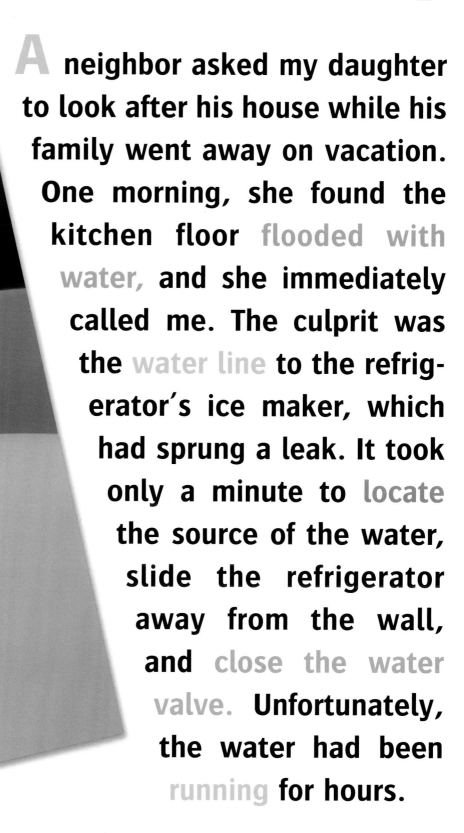

A neighbor asked my daughter to look after his house while his family went away on vacation. One morning, she found the kitchen floor flooded with water, and she immediately called me. The culprit was the water line to the refrigerator's ice maker, which had sprung a leak. It took only a minute to locate the source of the water, slide the refrigerator away from the wall, and close the water valve. Unfortunately, the water had been running for hours.

Good Water In, Bad Water Out

basically, your home's water is supplied by a pressurized water system provided by the city or your water company, or you may have an electric water pump if you have a private well. Over time, pressurized incoming water can present leak problems for appliances, faucets, and supply pipes. Outgoing wastewater, from drains and toilets, is not under pressure and simply flows out of the house by way of gravity—or so it's supposed to. But sometimes drains and pipes become clogged. When that happens, you've got a backup problem.

Good Water In ... Remember the Main!

Two of the most important things to know about your house are the location of the water main and how to shut off your home's main water-supply line. This could play a vital role in sparing your home major water damage in the event of a broken water pipe or other major water-related emergency.

The main water-supply line enters your home through the foundation and below the frost line. At this point or at your home's water meter (if you have municipal water) is where you should find the main water shutoff valve. Some meters may be located outdoors, underground. If that's the case with yours, find and lift the small metal cover to get at it.

It's a good idea to test the main shutoff valve once a year by opening and closing it just to make sure it's in good working order. But don't force the valve if it doesn't turn easily. Invest some money and have a plumber inspect, repair, and replace it if necessary.

You should also know where all the water shutoff valves are located in your home—on the wall below the toilet tank, under the sinks, near the washing machine, behind the refrigerator (if there is an automatic ice maker), and on the water heater. There will also be indoor valves for the outdoor water spigots attached to your house.

what would you do?

WATER, WATER EVERYWHERE

Water is pouring out from under your kitchen sink. The floor will look like a swimming pool soon if you can't stop the water. Would you

◄ a. call 911

◄ b. try to stop the leak with tape

◄ c. first, shut the water valve under the sink. Then, if you can't locate and repair the leaky pipe yourself, call a plumber

◄ d. shut the main water valve, and call a plumber

If your faucet or dishwasher started leaking severely, you should follow the advice of "c." You could also close the main valve, but that will cut off the water supply to the entire house, and that may not be necessary. Two copper pipes coming up through the cabinet floor, one for hot water (left) and one for cold (right), are located inside the cabinet beneath the sink. Each pipe will have a shutoff valve.

SHUTOFF VALVES

When repairing or replacing a leaky water pipe—or a faucet or fixture, for that matter—knowing where and how to shut off the water supply, either at the unit under repair or at the main water supply, is important. Turn off both the hot- and cold-water valves. Your dishwasher most likely hooks into the hot-water line under the kitchen sink and might have a separate shutoff, allowing you to use the sink's faucet even if the appliance is out of order.

In older homes, the valves look like wheels. Remember: turn each one clockwise (right) to close and counterclockwise (left) to open. In newer homes, a valve will have a handle instead of a wheel. When the handle is perpendicular, or at a 90-degree angle, to the pipe, making an "L," the valve is closed. When the handle is parallel with the pipe, the valve is open.

Bad Water Out— Thank You, Gravity!

h ave you ever noticed that if you quickly flip an open bottle of soda pop upside down, the liquid inside doesn't spill out immediately? Vapor lock prevents it. But puncturing the bottom of the overturned bottle breaks the vacuum, allowing gravity to pull the fluid down and out.

Your home's plumbing system acts in a similar manner. A vent on the roof of the house lets air and sewer gases move freely, preventing vapor lock and allowing gravity to force the wastewater down and out into the sewer system. Venting is an essential part of your overall plumbing system.

A drain trap is underneath a sink and resembles the letter P upside down. By retaining a residual amount of wastewater, the trap blocks unpleasant sewer gases from backing up through the drain and rising into your kitchen or bathrooms. However, these drain traps can also trap other things, such as dirt, hair, and diamond rings. That's how they become clogged. If you notice a musty smell coming from a sink, waste-disposal unit, shower, bathtub, or dishwasher, that may indicate a buildup of sediment and bacteria inside the pipe.

You need to treat these foul-smelling drains (not the toilet) with an enzyme-based cleaner. Treat them every day for a week; once a week for a month; and then once a month ongoing.

i didn't know that...

ROUTINE CHECKUP

Occasionally, take out all of that junk from under the sink—kitchen and bathroom—so that you can check the cabinet floor for moisture. Water from a slow-leaking faucet, pipe connection, gasket, or seal around the sink could be seeping into the cabinet, or worse, into the wooden subfloor under the cabinet. Insects just love soft, moist wood.

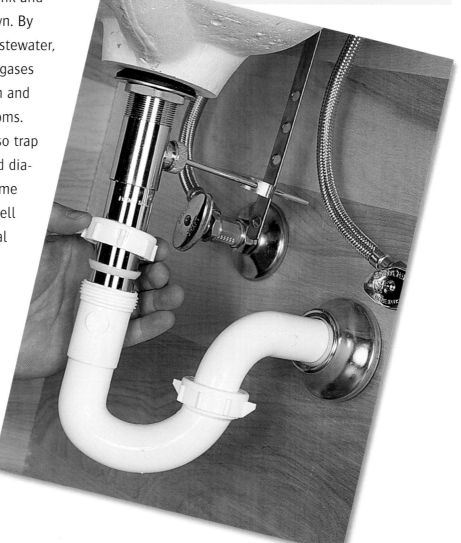

Sink Plungers

A drain plunger pushes the standing water downward into the obstruction and then creates a return vacuum when you pull up the plunger, often freeing the clog on the first try. Make sure the overflow vents, and the second drain on a double-bowl sink, are closed or sealed up with a rag before you attempt to plunge. Otherwise, the forced water or air will simply escape out of the vent. If the drain doesn't have enough standing water to create the push-and-pull vacuum, add some!

You can also find an aerosol plunger in any hardware or home-improvement store. It's like the air horn used by the crazy fans at the football game, only without the sound. As with the standard type of drain plunger, make sure the overflow vent or second drain is closed. Place the device into the standing water, and cover the drain to create an air seal. As you push the can downward, it releases a blast of compressed air into the drain, usually freeing the clog. Be careful, however, because the air pressure could blast water out of the sink. Place towels around the sink and floor, just in case.

A PLUGGED DRAIN, NOW WHAT?

OK, so you washed one too many hairs down the bathroom sink, and you've got a clogged drain. Now what? There are several things you can do to correct the problem. If the drain is simply running slowly, try pouring boiling water into it to clear the obstruction. If that doesn't work, remove the pop-up plug, and then use needle-nose pliers to dig out the clog. Then replace the plug.

You can also try using a liquid drain cleaner, which you can find in the supermarket. Many experts recommend not using them because they are caustic. You should be careful, and don't use the plunger if the liquid drain cleaner has not released the clog immediately. Splashes can be dangerous, especially if these chemicals get into your eyes. Give them time to work, and the standing water should disappear.

DEALING WITH BATH SINK POP-UPS

If you have to remove the pop-up plug in a bathroom sink to get to a clog, don't worry, it's easy. You'll have to lift the lever under the basin to free the plug. Here's how.

1 Loosen the nut securing the lever to the back of the drain tube under the basin, and pull the lever out partway.

2 Lift the pop-up plug. You may see a clump of hair clinging to it. Shine a flashlight into the drain, and retrieve the clog using a needle-nose pliers or a piece of wire that has been bent into a small hook on its end.

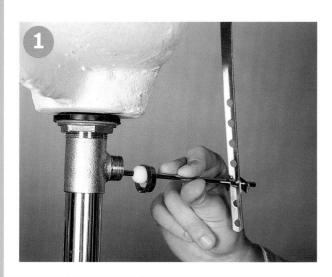

HOW TO UNCLOG OR "SNAKE" A SINK DRAIN

If you can't remove a clog using the methods discussed previously, you may have to remove the trap to get at the source of the problem. To do this, you'll need a wrench (unless the system is plastic, in which case you can unscrew the nut by hand), a pail or bucket, and a drain auger. None of these are expensive or difficult to find. Actually, they will come in handy more than once. Here's what to do.

1 To gain access to a sink drain, remove everything from under the sink, and place a bucket under the trap. Unscrew the nuts on the trap and trap arm. Plastic is hand tight, while chrome requires a wrench to loosen the nuts.

2 The drain line will most likely lead to the wall of the cabinet (below). Feed the auger cable into the pipe until you feel resistance; then crank through the clog clockwise, forward, and back. Once you break through the clog, reassemble the trap.

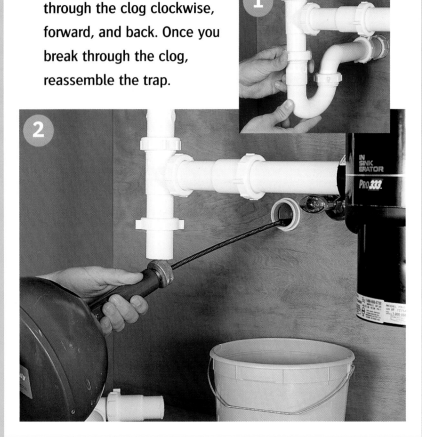

i didn't know that...

TOILET-TANK SWEATING

Is there water on the floor around the toilet? Toilet-tank sweating (condensation) is caused by a significant difference between cooler water temperature inside the water tank and the warmer air temperature inside the house. Most often, this can be corrected by inserting a thin insulating liner around the inner walls of the tank. This insulated liner can be found in any plumbing or home-improvement store.

Clogged Toilets

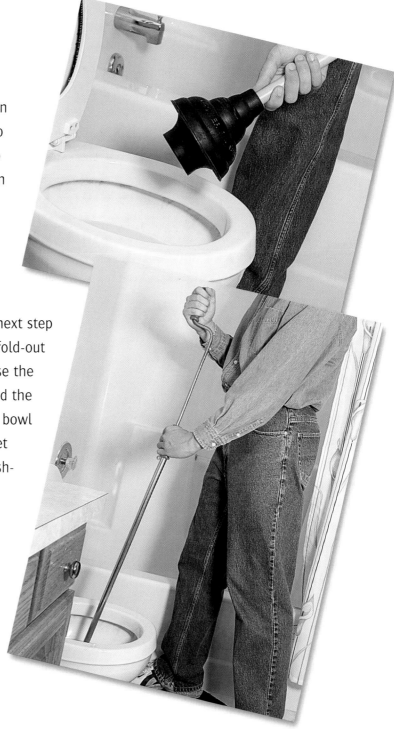

do not re-flush a clogged toilet if the water in the bowl is not at its normal level. Doing so will only cause the water to rise and overflow onto the floor. If the toilet starts to overflow, reach down underneath the toilet tank and shut the water-supply valve.

Often, the only thing you need to unclog a plugged toilet is time. Give whatever is clogging the toilet an hour or so to soften and become less dense and it might simply flush away. If not, your next step is to pull out the toilet plunger—the one with the fold-out cup. The up-and-down plunging motion might cause the bowl water to splash. Place some old towels around the toilet to protect the floor, and drape the top of the bowl with an old towel, holding it in place with the toilet seat. When using a plunger, make sure you are pushing water downward into the trap. This downward water thrust is what frees the clog. Some people argue it's the upward motion, but not in my book.

If the bowl doesn't contain enough water to plunge, open the water-supply valve, and then flush the toilet to add some. Keep an eye on the water in the bowl, and when it reaches a normal level, close the supply shutoff valve again. Then start plunging.

When the Plunger Doesn't Work

At this point, you'll have to call in the heavy artillery—the closet auger. Pull the handle and cable back, and inset the bend into the outlet at the bottom of the bowl. Slowly push the cable forward while cranking in a clockwise direction. When the crank handle bottoms out, retrieve the cable, and repeat the process. Run the cable through at least three times, forcing it left, right, and center. If the blockage is in the toilet, this will most likely take care of the problem.

Once the bowl water level returns to normal, or after the clog is cleared, open the water-supply valve. But if you have tried all of the above and the toilet is still clogged, it's time to call a plumber. You've got a bigger problem than you can handle.

CLIMATE CONTROL

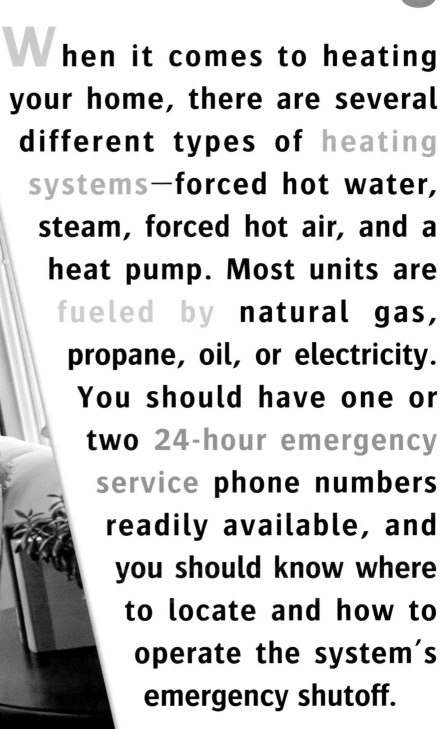

When it comes to heating your home, there are several different types of heating systems—forced hot water, steam, forced hot air, and a heat pump. Most units are fueled by natural gas, propane, oil, or electricity. You should have one or two 24-hour emergency service phone numbers readily available, and you should know where to locate and how to operate the system's emergency shutoff.

Have a professional inspect your system annually. Ask where the shutoffs are located. If you have an older *steam system*, which is designed to lose water over time, find out how and when to add the appropriate amount of water. If your *forced-hot-air furnace's* air handler contributes as part of the central air-conditioning system, have the system serviced in the spring and in the fall; during the summer, if the small pipe at the bottom of the air handler drips water, it's just the chiller unit creating condensation—it's normal. Lastly, modern burners are designed not to fire up when ventilation has been blocked, so if the burner has shut down after a heavy snowstorm, check to see whether the flue has been covered by snow.

Better Indoor Air

If you have a forced-air heating system, you probably also have an air filter attached to the return-air duct. The bottom of the furnace is where air is returned to the unit after having been circulated throughout the house. A metal or plastic box that holds the air filter is typically located between the furnace and the return-air duct.

Changing the filter yourself every four to six months is easy. Write down the model number of the filter, and head for the local home-improvement store to find the matching one. The directions for changing the filter should be described on the package. If not, pay close attention as you remove the old filter, and insert the new one the same way. (The same is true for a central-air-conditioning air filter.)

Reversing Dry Air

Your forced-air heating system might also be equipped with a central humidifier attached to the return-air duct. This appliance adds moisture to the warm air during the dry winter months by taking fresh water, running it through a delivery device, like a cylindrical foam pad or sponge, and then forcing air through the device to create a humid mist that is carried into the air via the duct system.

The fresh water is supplied by a small copper tube that taps into one of the home's fresh-water lines. Familiarize yourself with the location of this water line and the shutoff. As always, turning the valve to the right stops the flow of water during summer or if a malfunction occurs.

hot water

i didn't know that...

WHY ARE ROOMS A DIFFERENT TEMPERATURE?

If you have a forced-hot-air system and find that some rooms are hotter or colder than others, try adjusting the vents or register openings. Also, leaving the blower-fan motor on at all times helps balance the air temperature and airflow throughout the house. You might think that this will burn out the motor faster, but many HVAC contractors actually recommend running the motor constantly over periodic starting and stopping. Keep in mind that, even if the fan is running all the time, the heat or the air conditioning is not. Heating or cooling will automatically start as the home's temperature calls for it. The fan is simply moving around the air in the house.

heats up in-line towel warmers, too

The Water Heater

hot water delivered to your faucets is heated by some form of a heater. If you have a boiler, your domestic hot water may be provided by the home's hot-water or steam heating system. There might even be a separate standby tank for holding extra hot water so you're less likely to run out during a long shower. There is little for you to do or check with a system such as this.

If you have a forced-air heating system, you have a standalone water heater. These heaters typically look like the body of the Tin Man in *The Wizard of Oz*. Fueled by electricity, fuel oil, or natural gas, a water heater (and a standby tank) allows you to control the water temperature by adjusting a thermostat on the unit. For gas units, there is even a vacation setting that keeps only the pilot flame going to restart the system. (A pilot light kick-starts the major gas flame when the unit calls for heat.)

Run the hot water from your kitchen faucet, and place a thermometer into the flow. A typical water-temperature setting is 120 degrees Fahrenheit. The water heater's tank holds the hot water at temperature until hot water is used somewhere in the house. The heated water is then replaced with water coming in from the street service. When this unheated water enters the tank, the overall water temperature lowers, which signal's the unit's thermostat to initiate the heating process again.

KEEPING IT CLEAN AND SAFE

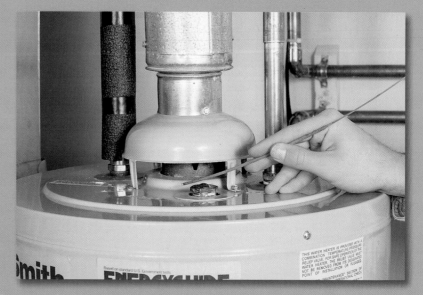

If your water heater is not self cleaning, drain a gallon bucket of water from the bottom spigot every six months to help the system last longer. However, you have to do this religiously, starting with a new unit, or don't bother. Stirring up all that sediment and muck may clog up faucets and shutoff valves. Also, in case the flue is clogged, it's a good idea to check for escaping carbon monoxide, which is deadly. (Install a carbon monoxide detector near the water heater and heating-system burner.) Hold a smoking match or an incense stick about 1 inch away from the flue hat (above). If the flue draws in the smoke, all is well.

what would you do?

A LEAKING TANK

You go downstairs to the basement (where your water heater happens to be located) to do the laundry. Uh-oh, there's water all over the floor—and it's coming from your water heater. Would you

◀ a. turn off the water valves attached to the water heater

◀ b. call a plumber?

The correct answer is "a," but you might also need a plumber. On the side of the water heater near the top, there is a temperature-and-pressure (T&P) relief valve, usually with a long vertical discharge pipe that almost reaches the floor. The valve is designed to pop open if the internal tank temperature or pressure reaches a dangerous level. If this happens, you'll have a mess on your hands unless the overflow pipe is near a floor drain.

Turn off the water heater by cutting off its electrical power—usually a light switch on or near the unit—or, if the water heater is gas-fired, turning the thermostat down to the "pilot" level (which is a two handed job, by the way). If possible, shut the water valves on both pipes that come out of the top of the water heater. If you can't locate these valves, turn off the water at the main water supply.

If the temperature of the water was simply set too high, reset the thermostat to the normal level, let things cool down for a couple of hours, restart the unit, and watch it carefully. If the thermostat was set correctly, then either the thermostat or the T&P relief valve is faulty. If this is the case, call in a professional to look over the system.

You will need to reignite the pilot flame of a gas-fired water heater. The directions should be clearly marked on the outside of the unit, and you must follow them exactly. A long-stemmed propane lighter will help this process. Another (less stressful) option is to simply call your utility service company. For a fee, they will come out and restart the water heater or gas furnace and then probably inspect the units.

If the water heater is 10 years old or past its warranty period, plan on replacing it—before it begins to fail and leak water into your home. For this, you should call a licensed plumber. In fact, in many locations you are required to do this and to get a permit from your municipality's building department. If you are replacing the water heater or buying new because you're building a home, inquire about one of the new, super-efficient, high-tech, tankless water heaters, which heat water only on demand (rather than maintaining 50 gallons of hot water at all times).

APPLIANCES

Modern appliances certainly make life easier, but they usually require a little maintenance to keep them working efficiently. With some care, you can also stretch the lifespan of most of them— a cost-saving move that's good for the environment, as well. When you buy a new appliance, take the time to read the manual, paying attention to the recommendations for maintenance. Just like cars, most appliances run better if you routinely service them.

The Refrigerator

the refrigerator is probably the most power-hungry appliance in your kitchen, if not in your home. To check its setting, place a thermometer in a glass of water and put the glass in the refrigerator. Wait a couple of hours, and then check the thermometer; it should read between 37 and 40 degrees Fahrenheit—no higher, and any lower is a waste of energy.

There are other things you can do to make your refrigerator run more efficiently. If you have a choice, don't locate it next to the range or dishwasher or near an outside door or window. These locations raise the ambient air temperature around the appliance, making it work harder to maintain a cool temperature.

Your refrigerator has a heat-exchanger coil much like your car's radiator located underneath or in back of the unit. This coil is designed to diffuse heat and must be kept free of dust by vacuuming it at least every six months. Removing the bottom kick-plate grille, held in place by spring clips, should expose coils (unless they are in back of the appliance) and a plastic moisture evaporator pan. Home-improvement stores sell a specially designed brush and an attachment for your vacuum cleaner for cleaning these coils.

Troubleshooting

Most refrigerators are frost-free, which means there is a mechanism in place that automatically removes moisture from the freezer and transfers it to an evaporator pan located at the bottom of the appliance. If you notice water coming out from the bottom of the refrigerator, that's not a good thing. There is a problem with either the defrost mechanism or the ice maker. (See "Leaky Ice Maker Water Line," on the opposite page.)

Check the freezer to see whether the temperature is rising. Remove the toe-kick grille to see whether the evaporator pan is overflowing. If either of these conditions exists, move food to another refrigerator, a cooler, or your neighbor's refrigerator because you've got a problem.

LEAKY
ICE-MAKER WATER LINE

If your refrigerator has an ice maker, it will have a water-supply hose that is attached to a valve on the wall behind the appliance. The valve looks similar to an outdoor water valve, and it turns on and off in the same way. If you can, roll the refrigerator away from the wall to allow access to the back of the unit.

Feel the water-supply line at its lowest point for wetness. If there is water, one of three things could be leaking: the valve, the hose connection at either end, or the hose itself. Using a flashlight and dry hands, try to determine what's causing the problem.

If you notice moisture coming from the top of the wall valve itself, call a plumber. You can try to tighten the connections to the hose from either the valve or the refrigerator——but don't force it too hard. If that doesn't work, plan on replacing the old hose.

To replace the hose, first shut the water-supply line. Then disconnect the hose from the back of the refrigerator, and let the water in the tube run into a pail. Once the hose is empty, disconnect the other end. Attach the new hose at both ends, first wrapping the threads on the connectors with pipe-thread tape to create a watertight seal, and you are done.

If the refrigerator is past its prime—8 or more years old—apply the repair money toward the purchase of a new unit. Most appliance stores offer a same-day or next-day delivery and setup service, and they will usually remove the old appliance. Tip the delivery guys some coffee money, and they might take away that old window air conditioner that's been lying around, too.

Front-loading washers and dryers should last almost a dozen years, especially if you maintain them properly.

i didn't know that...

A CLEAN LINT TRAP

Fabric-softener sheets can cause a film to form over the mesh of the lint trap. This creates a blockage that reduces the dryer's effectiveness and can burn out the dryer's heating element—or worse, cause a fire. So remove the lint trap every couple of months, and scrub it clean using an old toothbrush and soapy hot water.

The Clothes Washing Machine and Dryer

your clothes washing machine is connected to hot- and cold-water supplies by two reinforced rubber hoses that are under pressure at all times. You should open and close the water shutoff valves after each use, but as a practical matter, most homeowners don't. However, at least make a practice of closing the water supply if you plan to leave the house unattended for any length of time—particularly when you leave for extended trips or vacations.

Frequent use of these valves keeps them in good working order and helps make changing the hoses a simple task. I suggest replacing both hoses at least every two years. Remember to use pipe thread-sealing tape to create a watertight seal.

Why Aren't These Clothes Dry?

If you have an electric dryer and the unit just doesn't seem to be getting hot enough to thoroughly dry your clothes, the heating element may have gone bad. It can be replaced. But depending on the age of the unit and the cost of a service call, a better idea might be to buy a new dryer. If the dryer operates using gas, I wouldn't fool with it. Call in a serviceman or, once again, based on the age of the unit, apply that money toward the purchase of a new gas dryer.

GO AHEAD AND VENT

A dryer vents hot air and lint outside your home through an exhaust hose and vent. Over a period of time, lint builds up inside the exhaust hose, causing a reduction in the dryer's efficiency. Most home-improvement stores sell a dryer vent brush that loosens and removes lint from the hose and the vent. At least once a year, remove the lint from the vent or replace the exhaust hose with a new one. (See "Installing a Dryer Vent and Hose," on page 88.)

INSTALLING A **DRYER VENT AND HOSE**

If you don't have one, a dryer vent is not difficult to install. If you need to replace an old one, the following information will be helpful to you, too. Clothes dryers are lightweight and should move away from the wall without much effort. The vent hose can be made of plastic or metal. Plastic is easier to attach, but metal is best for fire protection. The hose connects to the back of the dryer with a simple circular spring clamp.

If you have to replace an old hose, squeeze the two ends of the clamp toward each other. If necessary, use pliers, but you may be able to do this with your hands. The clamp will expand allowing you to remove and replace the hose.

To install a dryer vent to the outside where one has not previously existed, you'll need a saber saw, a screwdriver, a dryer vent, flexible duct, a vent hood with damper, duct clamps, and caulk. Here's what to do.

1 Pick a spot between the wall studs. Trace and cut a hole the diameter of the vent hose.

2 Transfer your cuts through the interior and exterior walls. Mount the vent hood on the exterior.

3 Indoors, fit one end of the flexible duct over the vent cover pipe, and attach it using duct clamps.

4 Install the other end over the dryer outlet in back of the appliance using duct clamps. Try to avoid making severe bends or kinks in the new hose.

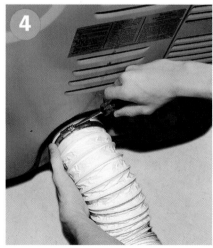

Water Softeners

if you have a private well or live in an area where the domestic water has a high mineral content, also known as "hard water," you may need (or have) a water-softening system. (If you have municipal water, call your water department and ask whether it provides pre-softened water; if so, you may not need a water softener.) Softening the water with salt (which is never introduced directly into the water, so there is no taste) helps reduce mineral scaling that can clog dishwashers and other appliances. Soft water promotes soap suds when showering or washing your clothes. (If you have reddish stains on sinks and toilets, use "iron-reducing" softener salt in your system.)

The degree of mineral content in the water determines the salt consumption settings of the water softener—this was established during the initial installation. However, things can change. You can test the hardness of your water using a special kit containing litmus paper, which changes color in the water. Matching the color of the litmus paper against a color scale indicates what the softener's setting should be, and the settings determine the amount of salt consumption. If you can't find the original manufacturer's documentation, you might have to contact them online or by phone.

Obviously, the higher the salt setting, the higher the consumption will be (but still with no "salt" taste) and the more frequently the salt reservoir must be refilled. Check it twice a month, and refill it accordingly. If the softener was out of salt for any extended period of time (more than a day or two), hit the button for the "regenerate" cycle. This will force the softener into the "on" mode.

i didn't know that...

A SOFT DRINK
Will softened water taste salty? No. Resin beads covered with sodium ions actually "soften" the water. The sodium ions come from brine created using softener salt. The brine is never introduced into your water.

The Cooktop or Range

keep your range or cooktop clean. Besides immediately wiping up spills and splatters on the cooktop, it's important to clean the burners, which can get pretty messy due to grease and caked-on grime. Use a nonabrasive cleaner, especially on electric coils. If you have a glass or ceramic cooktop, follow the manufacturer's directions for cleaning. Some detergents are too abrasive to use on ceramic or glass without damaging the surface. Warm water and mild dishwashing liquid will cut grease on most cooktops—and don't forget to clean the knobs or other controls.

Electric stovetop burner coils eventually wear out after prolonged use. These coils are much like large, circular, two-pronged wall plugs that pull out and plug back into an electrical outlet. Measure the diameter of the defective coil. You can find replacement coils in most home-improvement centers. If the heating element in an electric oven is faulty, it's not difficult to remove and replace that as well. Check the appliance owner's manual, which will tell you exactly what to do. If you don't have a manual, you can usually download a copy of it from the Internet. Go to the manufacturer's Web site, and if you know the model number of the appliance, you should be able to find the information you need. If not, call Customer Service.

what would you do?

COOKIN' RIGHT

It's a Sunday brunch with the girls. Quiche is on the menu and in the oven. Then the timer goes off. Mouth watering, oven mitts on, you open the oven door. Your quiche not only smells delicious, it looks...Wait a minute, what is this? Your quiche is custard-perfect around the edges, but it looks liquidy and uncooked in the center. Now what? Would you

◀ a. say, "heck, it tastes good anyway"

◀ b. check the oven owner's manual for trouble-shooting

◀ c. buy a new oven or range

◀ d. make sure the cord is plugged all the way into the outlet?

The best answer is "b," check the owner's manual, which may help you to pinpoint the problem. Uneven cooking is a sign that something is not right with the appliance. But before rushing out to replace it, make sure that the cord is securely plugged into the outlet ("d"). Check the gaskets around the oven door. If they are worn, heat will escape from the oven. You can probably find instructions for replacing them in the owner's manual. Also try repositioning the oven racks to see whether you get better results, and make sure the range is positioned evenly on the floor. In the end, you may have to call a repairman who may say that all he has to do is recalibrate the part that regulates the oven temperature—or he might tell you to start shopping.

most of today's faucets have

Fixing a Slow-Flow Faucet

at the end of most faucets is a round metallic housing that holds an aerator. An aerator's function is to direct water flow and introduce air into the stream that reduces splash-back. If you notice the water flow slowing down over time or if the spray pattern becomes irregular, the aerator may be clogged with mineral scaling and must be cleaned.

First, install the sink's drain stopper to prevent parts from falling down into the drain. Next, check to see whether the aerator's housing will unscrew with simple hand pressure. If not, wrap the housing with a strip of masking tape to protect the finish, and using pliers, unscrew it. Once the housing is removed, carefully note the disassembly sequence of the aerator's parts; you will have to reinstall them the same way.

Soak the parts in white vinegar to dissolve and remove the mineral scaling, and then scrub the parts with an old toothbrush. Trapped particles may have to be removed using the end of a needle or paper clip. If any of the parts have become brittle or broken, bring them to your home-improvement center and match them with a replacement.

After cleaning the aerator, reassemble and hand-tighten the housing on the faucet. Test for leaks around the threads. If one appears, use the pliers to retighten the housing until the leak stops. Remove the masking tape from the housing, and you're finished.

i didn't know that...

CONSERVE WATER
Replace the old aerator with one that has a flow rate of just 2.2 gallons per minute. Bring the old one to the store when you shop to make certain that you buy a new one that fits.

built-in flow-control devices

The Case of the Humming Waste-Disposal Unit

g reat! You have a waste-disposal unit, or garbage disposal, full of junk. You turn on the appliance, and all you hear is a humming noise, or worse, you hear nothing at all. Now what?

If you hear nothing at all, check for a blown fuse, a tripped circuit breaker, or a tripped ground-fault circuit interrupter (GFCI), as described in Chapter 7. Look underneath the sink to find the unit's red reset button. Try to solve the problem by pushing and releasing the red reset button, and see whether this solves the problem. If you are sure that the unit has electrical power (but you don't hear the humming noise, and the reset button doesn't do the trick), the disposal unit may have quit. It's time to have the unit repaired or replaced.

If you do hear humming, it means that the unit is getting electrical power and is most likely jammed. Make sure the power switch is in the "off" position. Remove the rubber sink strainer, and start pulling all that junk out of the unit.

Use a flashlight to see whether you can spot a foreign item that might be jamming the gears. If so, remove it using a pair of needle-nose pliers. Then turn on the disposal unit to check your work. If the humming noise continues, it's time for a repairman. If the unit is more than three years old, replace it.

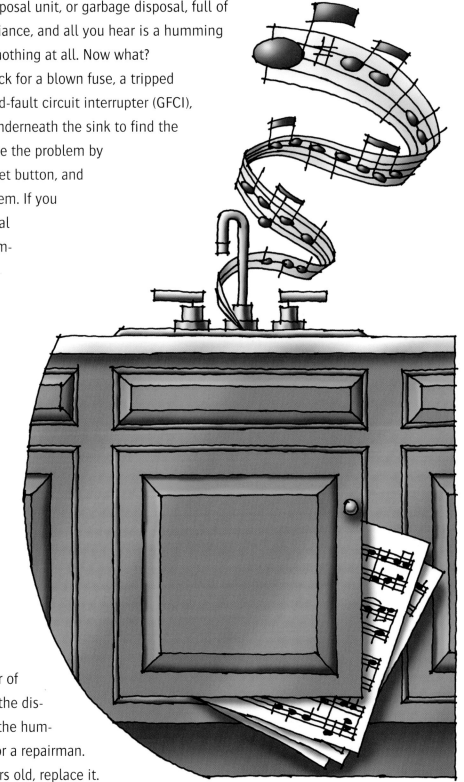

The Vacuum Cleaner... Keep It or Bag It?

acuum cleaners are simple devices with an internal fan that creates suction, pulling air through one end and expelling it at another. In between, it has a series of filters and a bag or canister to trap dirt and hair. Vacuum cleaners may have up to three separate filters, not including the collection bag. If you experience a drop in the effectiveness of your vacuum cleaner, make sure all the filters have been changed, or empty the canister. Even if the filters look clean, replace them. You might be pleasantly surprised at the improved performance.

If you're still unhappy with the appliance or if some other mechanical problem exists, based on the cost of a new model, consider bringing the old device into a repair shop for an estimate. This could save you money and give you back an appliance that is, basically, in like-new condition. But do this only once or twice, depending on the cost of the repair and the price of a replacement unit.

Getting a (Gas) Fireplace Going

having trouble starting a gas fireplace? Look for a round (brass) safety starter valve, embedded into the face of the fireplace. In the center of this valve you will notice a square key-hole. You will need the key, which is probably located on the mantelshelf to prevent children from accidentally turning on the gas. Look for any "open" or "closed" label forged into the top of the valve. But don't open the valve, which turns on the gas, yet.

Open the doors and cinder screen to the fireplace. Next, look for either a lever or a handle that opens the chimney flue (the metal door that, when open, permits venting of gases and smoke). When closed, the flue keeps downdrafts from entering the house. You can usually see whether the flue is open by looking up the chimney using a flashlight. If you're not sure, don't light the fire-place. Call in a chimney sweep or handyman to check it out first. Once you know the flue is open, step back from the unit and light a long match or a long-stem butane lighter. Remember, you have not turned on the gas yet.

While holding the match or lighter in one hand, move the flame into the fireplace, locating it at the center base of the ceramic logs. Now, with the other hand, open the gas safety valve by turning the key as you would a water faucet. Move the match or lighter flame horizontally all along the base of the ceramic gas logs. The gas should ignite within a few seconds.

If the gas-fired flame hasn't caught sufficiently within five sec-onds, extinguish it and immediately close the gas valve. Fan the area, and allow five minutes for the gas to dissipate. Then retry the process. If the gas doesn't ignite after several attempts, make sure the valve is shut and call a repairman.

Presuming the lighting was successful and you're finished enjoying your fire, close the valve. Leave the flue open overnight to make sure there are no smoldering embers or fumes to worry about. Depending on your model, leaving the flue open all night (or opening it at all) might not be necessary, but it simply provides peace of mind. Close the doors, and that's it.

INTER-VIEW WITH A CHIMNEY SWEEP

How can you tell whether you're hiring a reputable professional? Ask the chimney sweep for his or her certificate of liability insur-ance. Remember, this person will most likely be spending some time on your roof.

Also, ask about how and when to open and shut the flue, what type of wood to burn, how to prevent sparks from dam-aging your floor or rug, and whether to install a rain cap on the chimney, if only to keep birds from nesting inside during the spring.

i didn't know that...

SLEEPYTIME

By the way, do you feel sleepy when you've been sitting in front of a lit fireplace? Heat rises, and this upward draft depletes the room's oxygen. Take a look at the bottom middle of the glass-door frame. You might notice a decorative button or slide. This slide opens and closes a vent that allows you to control the rate of the burn by feeding the fire with more or less oxygen.

IN THE BASEMENT

A basement may offer extra storage and living space, but because it can be prone to moisture or flooding, you'll have to take measures to keep out water. One of the things you can do is seal the floors and walls. There are sealants on the market that are as easy to apply as paint. The other thing you can do is install a sump pump. Also, talk to your homeowner's insurance agent about coverage for a flood-ed basement—before it happens.

If the Sump Pump Fails

if your sump pump fails and the basement floods, contact your insurance agent immediately, and if you rent, also notify the property owner. A sump-pump failure caused by a power outage can often lead to a ruined finished basement. Every homeowner with a finished basement and electric sump pump should invest an extra $400 to $600 to have a battery-powered backup sump pump professionally installed. Also, a sump pump should have its own electrical circuit.

How a Backup Pump Works

If the battery backup pump kicks in, a loud, annoying warning alarm will alert you. If there was a power failure, most likely the power will return in a reasonable time. The main sump pump will resume its primary role, and the backup pump will go back to standby mode. Simply hit the reset button on the battery charger, and that's it.

If the battery backup alarm kicks in and there was no loss of electrical power, something happened to the main sump pump. You can hit the reset button to shut off the warning alarm, but if the backup pump has taken over, call a plumber immediately. A battery-powered backup pump is only good for as long as the life of the battery. It should be replaced at the end of its warranty or at least every four years.

Another option is a domestic water-driven backup pump. Ask your plumber about this.

HOW TO SEAL A CONCRETE FLOOR

This job requires no special skills. You'll need a scrub brush, bucket, sponge mop, mason's chisel or scraper, vacuum cleaner, paintbrush, hand-held sprayer, dust-mist respirator or dust mask, trisodium phosphate (TSP), and clear concrete sealer. Here's what to do.

1. Clean away stains and soiled areas using trisodium phosphate (TSP).

2. Scrape away any rough and uneven spots using a chisel or other steel-edged scraping tool.

3. Vacuum away concrete dust and other debris in cracks and joints that could reduce adhesion.

4. Using a paintbrush, apply a coat of clear concrete waterproofing sealer around the perimeter of the floor.

5. Evenly spray the sealer on the remainder of the floor.

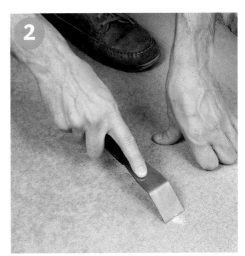

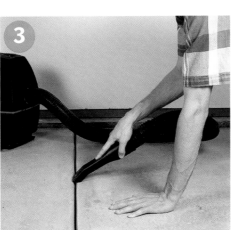

i didn't know that...

Flooded Basement

before anything like this happens, check with your insurance agent to make sure you have a homeowner's policy that covers a flooded basement.

What you do to recover from a flooded basement depends on the severity of the problem and your personal capabilities. It's not enough to simply remove the water. You must also correct the cause of the flooding and thoroughly dry out the basement to prevent the development of dangerous mold, usually first seen as black dots or spots.

Finished walls, insulation, rugs, and padding all act like sponges, and correcting even a mildly flooded basement is a multiperson undertaking. If the flooding or damage is severe, you should call in a professional remediation service. The pros will remove the water, fix the reason the flood occurred, and initiate the drying-out processes.

However, if you plan on tackling this yourself, you must take safety precautions. Make sure someone is with you or knows where you are and what you're doing in case of an emergency. Walking into a wet, flooded basement in your bare feet or without rubber boots is crazy. Stay away from the electrical service panel until the basement is completely dry.

For electrical power, connect a heavy-duty extension cord to an upstairs outlet, and string it up so that it doesn't lie in standing water. With rubber boots and dry feet, rubber gloves and dry hands, unplug the sump pump from its wall outlet, and then plug it into the extension cord. If that doesn't start the pump, either the pump motor or the mercury float switch is bad and must be replaced. If the sump pump does start, something else must have happened to the pump's electrical circuit, such as a blown circuit breaker or fuse.

If all that's left to do is remove a minimal amount of water, you will need a wet-dry shop vacuum and a number of trips to dump the water. With the water removed, the drying must begin. You will need to borrow, rent, or buy a couple of powerful circulating fans, at least one dehumidifier, and some air sponges (charcoal canisters that absorb musty odors). Most rental outlets are very familiar with your problem and will have all the equipment you will need.

If the rug has a pad, pull the rug edges away from the wall and any thresholds. You must get the blowing air from the circulating fans to flow in between the rug and the pad. If you can dry out the basement quickly and well enough, you will avoid a mold problem. But watch it closely. If mold eventually appears on the wall, you may have to replace the drywall and insulation. Hire a professional for this.

GOIN' OUTDOORS

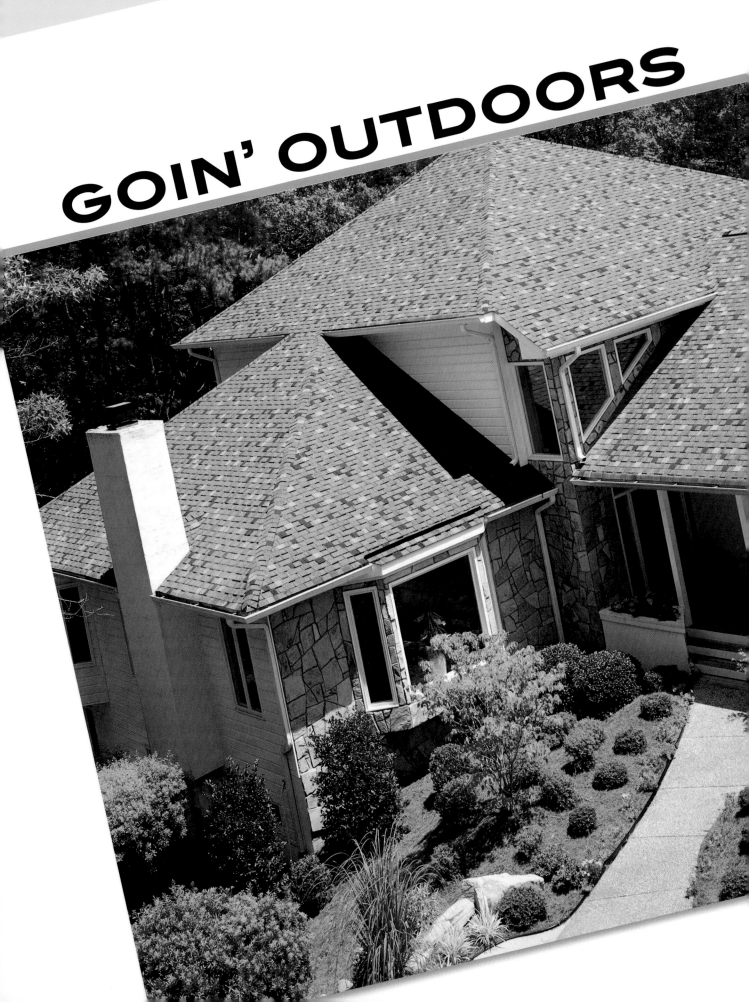

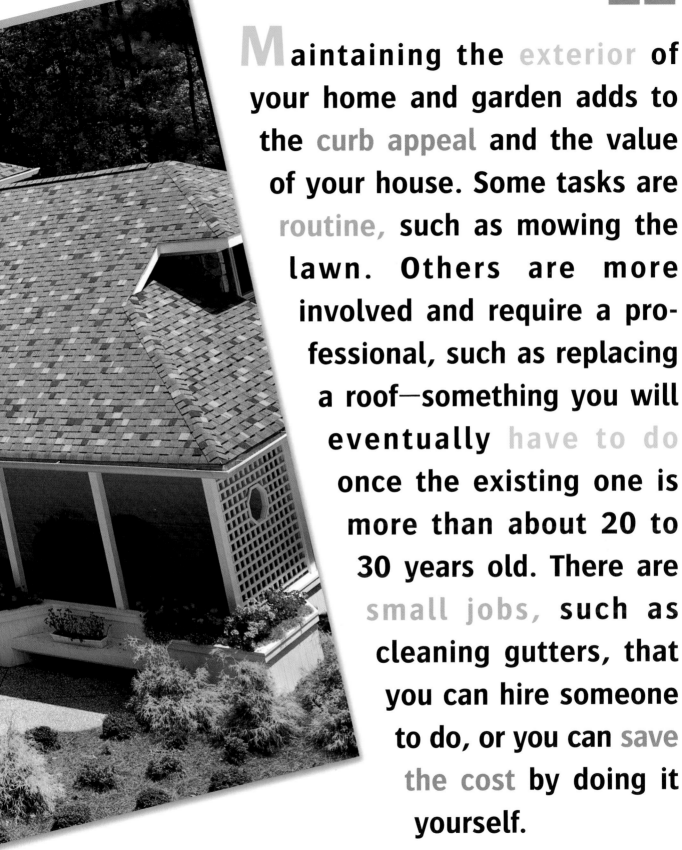

Maintaining the exterior of your home and garden adds to the curb appeal and the value of your house. Some tasks are routine, such as mowing the lawn. Others are more involved and require a professional, such as replacing a roof—something you will eventually have to do once the existing one is more than about 20 to 30 years old. There are small jobs, such as cleaning gutters, that you can hire someone to do, or you can save the cost by doing it yourself.

Roof and Gutters

if you notice a missing roof shingle, don't panic. When roofing shingles are installed, they are layered in overlapping rows to reduce the chance of leakage. So what you see as a missing shingle is more likely just a missing bottom tab of a shingle on the upper layer, and it probably will not pose an immediate leak problem, because there is another layer just below it. With just a little aluminum flashing and roofing cement, replacing the missing tab, or that particular shingle, would be just fine as a long-term repair. Be wary of any contractor who uses the missing shingle tab to try to sell you an entirely new roof.

How do I know whether I need a new roof?

Even a leaky roof does not necessarily mean a new roof is on the agenda. The leak could be related to other factors, such as worn aluminum chimney and vent flashing, snow and ice dams forming on the roof, backed-up gutters, or bad skylight seals. When an old roof really starts to give way, you might notice a significant amount of shingle granules washing off the roof into the gutters and through the down spouts. Other telltale signs include curling or cupping of the shingles, or multiple shingle tabs falling off the roof.

If you're uncertain, ask a certified home inspector to come by and give your roof a close examination. It might cost you a few dollars because he doesn't sell roofs, but you'll get an honest answer, and it might save you some money in the long run.

If you do need a roof, ask the inspector about placing the new roof directly over the old roof. If the local building codes allow it, and the old shingles don't have any major curling, laying a second roof over the first will save you the cost of having the old shingles removed. This is a common practice, and it costs less.

HOW TO HIRE A
ROOFING CONTRACTOR

Obtain three written bids from well-respected roofing contractors who have been in business for at least three years. Ask your contractor about the experience of the labor crew who will perform the work and get references.

Also, make sure the contractor you choose gives you a copy of his company's liability insurance coverage (which should be at least a million dollars, preferably more) before the work begins. No proof of coverage, no work! You have the right and obligation to protect yourself. If you don't, it could cost you much more than just a roof.

Never pay any contractor in full until the work is completed correctly. If you do, you cease to be a priority, and the work will take longer or never get finished. A successful contractor shouldn't need a prepayment arrangement—unless the materials are custom made. If you agree to this, don't pay anything until you see the materials delivered to the job site.

Whatever the terms, hold back at least 25 percent as final payment upon the completion of the work, which includes cleaning up the site. If the contractor complains he needs more money to pay his crew, that's his problem, not yours. This is a signal that corners might be cut. If your relationship with your contractor has become strained, consider calling in a certified home inspector to review the work before you make your final payment.

Gutters

A clogged gutter can force water and ice to back up under the roofing shingles, causing severe structural damage to a roof.

A quick way to determine whether a gutter is clogged is to simply put on a raincoat during heavy rain and observe the flow of each downspout. If a gutter is badly clogged, you will notice a restricted flow and rainwater splashing over the tops of the gutter. Obviously, this is not an exact science.

The sure method is to make an appointment with a handyman or gutter-maintenance service each fall to have the gutters inspected and cleaned. Remember, whenever you have any contractor on a ladder or on your roof, make sure they first give you a certificate of their liability insurance.

Although a bit pricey, you could have a leaf-and-debris gutter screen installed. This will remove cleaning clogged gutters from the fall season "to-do" checklist.

If you prefer to clean the gutters yourself, home-improvement centers sell a tool that you can use to get the job done. It can be messy, however, so wear a raincoat and goggles.

i didn't know that...

DAMP BASEMENT?
A considerable amount of rainwater runs off your roof into your gutters and out the downspouts. To prevent water from entering your basement, install ground-level extensions to your downspouts that will channel rainwater away from the foundation of the house.

Repainting the exterior of your house can take years off its appearance and add value to the property.

Repainting Basics

before repainting the exterior of your house, you'll need to do some surface preparation, such as washing the siding and the trim. In fact, scrubbing with a solution of warm water and nonabrasive household detergent can sometimes be as effective as repainting.

If repainting is necessary, go over the surface and the trim with a light sanding. Then wash the siding because new paint won't adhere over dirt, mold, or other surface deposits, such as grease from a kitchen exhaust fan.

You can fill hairline cracks with paint, but caulk large openings, such as where the ends of siding butt against trimwork. Wherever you sand, scrape, set nails, or make other repairs that expose raw wood, prime the area before painting.

Limit yourself to working on one manageable area at a time, and always work from top to bottom. The paint will probably drip and splatter, but you can fix this on your way down.

PAINTING **A HOUSE**

Prepare thoroughly before starting an exterior painting project by making sure you have everything you need to get it done. In addition to a ladder and possibly scaffolding, you'll need a 4-inch paintbrush, a 1½-inch sash brush, a caulking gun, a hammer, a nail set, scrapers, a sanding block, exterior paint, caulk, putty, and sandpaper.

1. Use a nail set to recess popped nailheads below the surface of the siding.
2. Fill in nailholes and gaps with putty, and allow to dry; then sand the patches smooth.
3. Scrape old paint that is blistered or peeling.
4. Recaulk around windows and doors.
5. Spot-prime sanded and scraped areas and places that have been caulked and puttied.
6. Paint starting from the top. Pros apply one primer coat and two finish top coats.

Lawn and Garden

it's spring, and lawn fertilizer sales are everywhere. But you really should fertilize your lawn four times per year—in early spring, twice during the summer, and once again in the fall.

In the spring, use a fertilizer that contains a pre-emergent crab-grass and weed stopper. Apply it when the ground temperature reaches at least 55 degrees Fahrenheit, which is when weed spores germinate. Putting down a pre-emergent fertilizer too early or too late will not be effective. Lawn areas abutting the street, walks, and sidewalks reach germination temperature a week or so earlier than the main part of the lawn. So the spring application requires a bit of strategic timing.

Plan on putting down the second application of a weed and feed fertilizer some time around the last week in May or the first week in June, depending on where you live. In midsummer, lawns need a fertilizer with an insecticide grub stopper (usually applied when you see Japanese beetles). Finally, in the late fall before a hard freeze, apply a winterizer fertilizer.

i didn't know that...

A GOOD TRIM
Keep the grass between 3 and 3½ inches tall to help prevent weeds from gaining hold—but don't cut more than one-third of the length per cut. Most lawn mowers have an independent height adjuster on each wheel.

Watering the Grass

Many homeowners have their own preferences, but I prefer to soak the lawn thoroughly a couple of times per week rather than just briefly spray it down every day. A thorough soaking aids in root development. Ideally, you should water the lawn early in the morning. Watering the lawn at night could lead to lawn fungus, and watering during the middle of the day causes excessive evaporation. Some experts believe the water acts as sun magnifier, burning the blades of grass. I'll buy it.

i didn't know that...

HOW MUCH FERTILIZER SHOULD YOU BUY?

That's a good question. First you have to know the size of your lawn. To calculate that in square feet of lawn, use this equation from junior high school: length x width = area.

Here's an easy way to approximate it. Let's say your walking stride is about 2.5 feet in length. Walk the north side of your lawn and count the paces—say 30, for example. Then, count your paces walking on the east side—25, for example. Now do the math.

Length (30 x 2.5) = 75 feet. Width (25 x 2.5) = 62.5 feet.

To find the area, or total square feet of lawn, multiply the length by the width. In my example, that's 75 x 62.5 = 4,688 square feet.

That means I would buy one bag that covers 5,000 square feet and use all of it.

By the way, you'll use a fertilizer spreader only four or five times a year. It's one more item taking up space in your garage or shed, but it's important for a healthy lawn.

what would you do?

HOW TO START A LAWN MOWER (OR OTHER GAS-POWERED ENGINES)

It's time to mow the lawn. For your lawn mower or any an engine to start, it needs:

◀ Fuel. Check the owner's manual, which should state whether your mower requires regular gas or a gas-and-oil mixture.

◀ Air. A cold engine must first be primed and choked. Find the choke-control lever, and move it to the "full" position. The choke-control is usually located on the handlebar as part of the throttle lever. Alternatively, it could be located directly on the engine as a lever that looks like an arrow pointing to the "full" direction. Next, locate the rubber primer button. This could be a black or red rubber button on the top or side of the engine, or it could be a black, red, or semitransparent plastic bubble or button located at the base of the carburetor. Push the primer button four or five times.

◀ Ignition. The spark plug creates a spark to start the engine.

Newer mowers have a safety kill-switch feature that looks like a second handlebar. In order to start the engine, this spring-loaded bar must first be squeezed against the larger handlebar and held in place while the engine is running. If you leave the mower unattended even for an instant, the bar releases, killing the spark and shutting down the engine.

Your new mower may be equipped with a battery and a key start. For the rest of us, the engine will have a pull-cord handle located either on the handlebar or on the engine. Pulling it generates a spark that ignites the fuel and starts the engine. Squeeze the kill-switch bar and the handle-bar together, and hold it with one hand. With the other hand, pull hard on the start cord. Repeat, and if the engine doesn't start after the fourth pull, push the primer button three or four times. Then retry the pull start.

A few seconds after the engine starts, pull the choke back from "full" to the "off" or "run" position. In colder weather, moving the choke back three-fourths or one-half might be necessary until the engine reaches a proper running temperature.

Finally, never start a gas engine in a closed garage, because gas engines emit dangerous carbon monoxide fumes.

Outdoor Water Spigots

Water expands when it freezes. An outdoor water-supply line full of trapped frozen water will easily split a copper water pipe, and you will have a major water leak on your hands. Unless you live in a climate that never freezes, close the shutoff valve that controls your outdoor water spigots, and drain them each fall. Older outdoor spigots must be manually drained from inside the house. Modern outdoor spigots are designed with a long stem that actually shuts off the water on the inside of the home's foundation. However, I simply don't trust them. I've seen too many freeze and split as a result of either improper installation or a leaky shut-off washer. I recommend closing the valves and draining them.

Winterizing (Draining) the Spigot

With an approximate sense of where the outdoor spigot is located, head for the basement with a flashlight, a pair of pliers, and a small bucket to catch water. Look just above the foundation wall for a copper pipe that seems to punch through the wooden sill that sits atop the concrete foundation.

You should notice a shutoff valve with a small bleeder-valve cap that looks very similar to a brass cap on an inner tube. Turn this valve clockwise to close it. Next, go back outside and turn on the outdoor spigot to release any air vapor lock. Then return to the basement.

Hold the bucket in position, and unscrew the bleeder-valve cap by turning it counterclockwise. You might need pliers to do this. The trapped water from the outdoor spigot will drain back into the home through the bleeder cap and into the bucket.

When the dripping stops, retighten the bleeder-valve cap; leave the indoor spigot closed but the outdoor spigot open. This will prevent any residual water from building up inside the pipe if the inside valve just happened to be the least bit faulty.

what would you do?

GARDEN HOSE LEAKS

You've just planted your vegetable garden, and you want to give it a good watering, but *you're* getting the hosing, not your zucchini. Would you

◀ a. replace the the washer gasket at the end of the hose

◀ b. put duct tape around the leak

◀ c. buy a new hose?

The best answer is "a." Fixing a leak at the faucet end or a leaky nozzle could be as simple as replacing a round washer gasket. These washers wear or dry out over time and begin leaking, and they should be replaced every new season.

Dig out the old washer using needle-nose pliers or a small flat-head screwdriver, and try to keep it intact for matching purposes. Most garden or home-improvement centers sell replacement hose washers, and they're very inexpensive. Just match the size you need, and push it into place, and that should cure any leaks.

By the way, I've found rubber garden hoses to be more durable and user friendly than plastic ones, particularly when rolling them up in colder weather.

ABOUT YOUR

part II

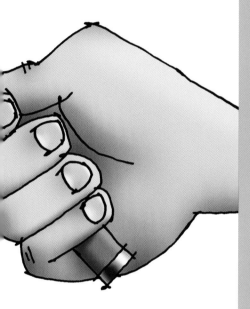

CAR

SHOPPING FOR A CAR

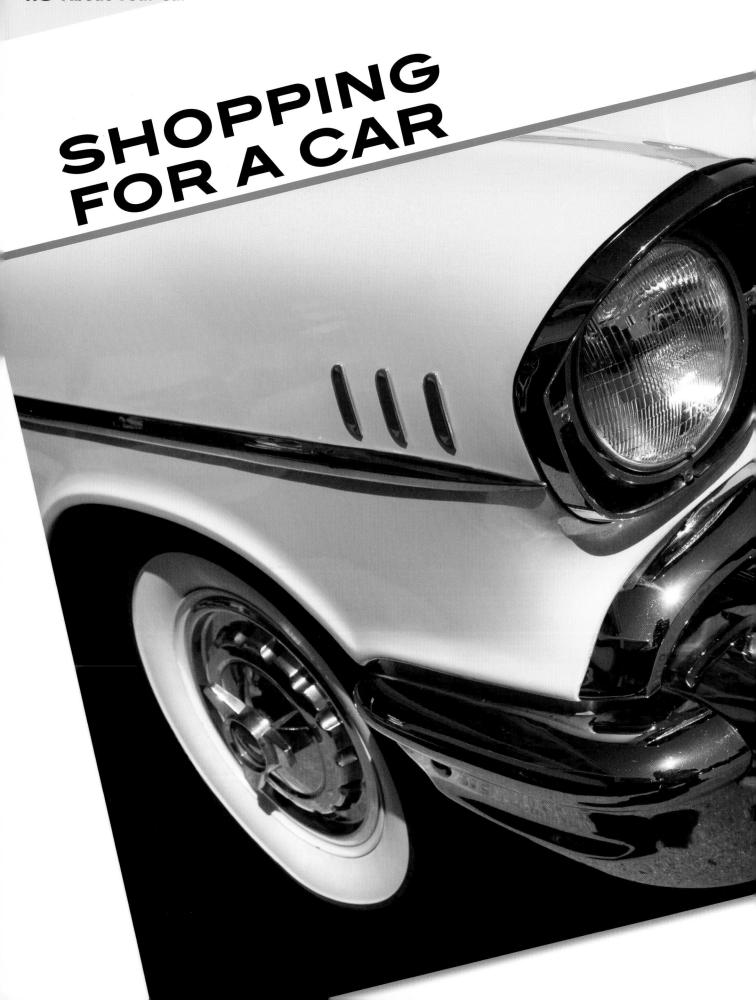

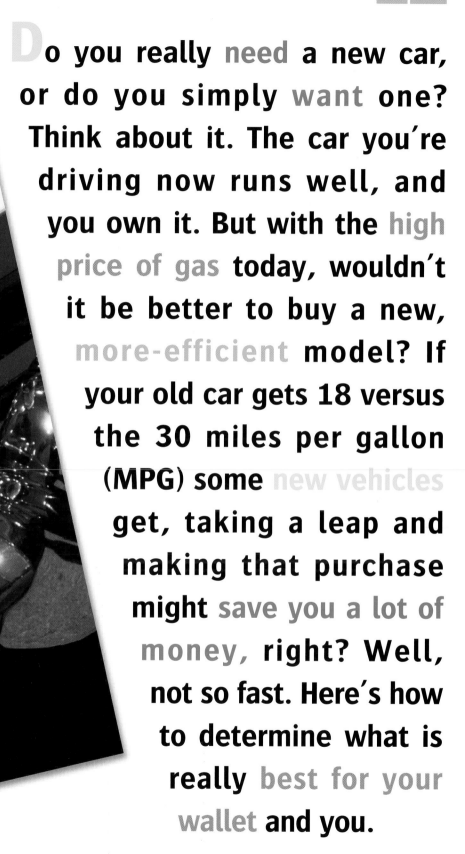

Do you really need a new car, or do you simply want one? Think about it. The car you're driving now runs well, and you own it. But with the high price of gas today, wouldn't it be better to buy a new, more-efficient model? If your old car gets 18 versus the 30 miles per gallon (MPG) some new vehicles get, taking a leap and making that purchase might save you a lot of money, right? Well, not so fast. Here's how to determine what is really best for your wallet and you.

Is Leasing for You?

depending on the car, lease payments could be $200 or more a month less than if you bought the car with a loan. If you choose to lease, save and invest the difference between the lease and loan payments. If you don't have the discipline to do this, leasing will be the more expensive option in the long run. On the other hand, the financial benefit of *buying* a car comes after you pay off the loan. How many years can you drive a car without a monthly loan payment, major repair bills, and lower car insurance rates? A lease could be for three or four years, and then you simply lease another new car. But if you bought a new car and took care of it, you could own it for another 6 to 10 years, which saves you a lot of money.

If you're still thinking of leasing a car, be careful. Pay close attention to the fine print. An advertised low monthly payment is usually offset by putting down thousands of dollars up front, representing a dealer-acquisition fee, a depreciation charge, and a lease-termination fee. Don't forget, you will also be charged if you go over the annual mileage amount stated in the agreement.

If you do decide to lease a car, all the same principles of buying a new car apply, including the rebates. The better you deal, the lower your lease.

LEASE OR BUY CHECKLIST

There are many arguments about whether it pays to lease or buy a car. What they boil down to is this: leasing is right if you
- want lower monthly payments, yet don't mind never reaching a final payment
- want to drive a new car every few years
- don't want the hassle of trading-in or selling an old car
- want to avoid major repair costs not under warranty
- agree to drive within a specified amount of miles
- don't care about owning equity in a car.

On the other hand, buy a car if you
- don't mind driving the same car for four or more years
- take pride in the upkeep of your car
- prefer to own something when you're through paying for it
- want a car that you could some day sell or trade
- drive more than about 12,000 miles a year
- enjoy making custom improvements to a car.

i didn't know that...

THE PRICE IS RIGHT

Your objective is to pay between 3 and 5 percent over what the dealer paid to the manufacturer for a specific car with those options—then add in the freight cost. Head for the bookstore, and pick up a new-car-buying guide. Do an online search of "How to Find Out What a Dealer Paid for a Car" and "Car Buying Tips." There are Web-based services that can help you obtain all of the up-to-date information about the car you're considering. Some may charge a small fee (about $10 per vehicle). But the information could be worth thousands of dollars to you. Print it, and take it with you to the dealership to negotiate your price. A quick measure is to buy your car at roughly 85 percent of the window sticker cost—before any cash-back incentives are mailed to you from the manufacturer.

Buying a New Car from a Dealer

the overall process of buying a car, from the start of the research to the final sale, should take anywhere from three to six weeks—not just a weekend afternoon. A car dealer has five tools to extract the most money from you: the window sticker price (also called the "Manufacturer Suggested Retail Price," or "MSRP"), trade-in value, financing through the dealership, extra add-ons, fees (registration and license plates, destination charges), and you. If you haven't done your homework, act too eagerly, feel too intimidated to say "no," or are not willing to walk away and search for a better deal, then either you don't care about money or you're a lamb heading for slaughter. Car dealers are masters of the deal, and you're on their turf.

Be Smart

Understand exactly what car and exactly what options you want. A car that interests you might also be a favorite among car thieves. Cars that are stolen more often carry a higher insurance premium. Talk with your insurance company or contact the National Insurance Crime Bureau for a list of the most frequently stolen vehicles over the past year.

Visit different dealerships; bring a camera and a notebook; but leave your checkbook and credit cards home. Look around the lot; open car doors; and sit inside. If you like a particular vehicle, make notes from the window sticker about its options and costs.

Don't let the salesperson talk and waste your time. Test-driving at this early stage is optional but time-consuming. Take the salesperson's business card. After you have narrowed down your choices, set up test-drive appointments. When you test-drive a car, the salesperson will likely ask for your license to photocopy it. If you don't want a credit check done, let the salesperson know that you do not want him or or her to use the license to do a check, which is *not* necessary for insurance purposes. An unauthorized credit check could be against the law, by the way.

Check out special promotions and factory-to-dealer incentives that give dealers more opportunity to reduce the price and still make a fair profit.

HIDDEN FEES AND COSTS

A cagey dealer will allow you to think you're getting a great deal and then, after you think the game is won and your guard is down, in come the hidden costs. Dealer prep charges, advertising fees, additional dealer mark-up fees, dock fees, and more are all a means for sucking out as much money from you as legally possible.

Before you begin any meaningful price negotiation, ask the dealer for a list of all the after-sale costs and fees that you should expect so you can compare the costs with other dealerships. All of these fees should be negotiated or waived, in writing, before any agreement takes place.

You should also know what your trade-in is worth. Chances are the dealer will offer you only one-third to one-half of what you would expect. Check out the *Kelly Blue Book Used Car Guide—Consumer Edition,* or check online. The dealership probably uses the same service. Based on the year, make, options, mileage, and condition of your vehicle, this book will suggest a wholesale and retail value. If your car is 5 years or older, chances are that the dealership won't want it and will offer you only a fraction of what it is worth as a private sale.

Making an Offer

Let the games begin. The salesperson will eventually ask you to make an offer. But it's the sales manager who is the approving authority and the guy behind the glass window you see flailing his arms and shaking his head over your first couple of offers. This is all part of the game, and when you recognize it, you will laugh.

While your first offer is being rejected, you will be left alone to stew and stress about whether you should have offered more money for the car, or so goes the sales strategy. Let them know you're not one to fret. When the salesperson leaves to present your offer, get up and walk around the showroom. Also, be careful. A private discussion you think you're having with your partner may be listened to via a telephone intercom speaker left

i didn't know that...

FINANCING

Know your credit-score rating. A credit rating under 650 can raise the finance rate or the annual percentage rate, (APR) and your loan could cost more. Speak with a loan officer at your local bank or credit union about your plans, and ask for their options or suggestions. You will receive good advice and have another arrow in your quiver when the time comes to review the dealer's financing recommendations.

on inadvertently. If you have offered 5 percent over cost, plus freight, and you don't have a deal, walk away. The salesperson will do everything except throw himself in the back of your car as you're leaving.

Do some research before buying a used car. Find out what you can about its history.

Buying a Used Car

Whether you're buying a used car privately or at a dealership, pick up a car-buying guide, such as the *Kelly Blue Book Used Car Guide—Consumer Edition,* or check online.

The advantage of buying a used car from a dealer is that the car has presumably been inspected, serviced, and cleaned. The tires will probably be in reasonable shape, and the car will carry some form of dealer warranty. The private sale, however, can be a real value if you know enough not to be taken. The question in either case is why this car has found its way to the sales block. Is there something wrong? Has the car been in a major accident?

A dealership probably obtained its vehicle through a trade-in, auction, or lease expiration. The private seller probably has found he couldn't get what the car is worth through a trade-in and has decided to sell it on his own. A private seller could also have personal circumstances that caused the sale, such as the need to get rid of Grandpa's old car, which could be a good value for you. But before you buy, you need to know about the car's history.

Do Some Detective Work

Ask how many previous owners the car had. I'd feel better if the seller is the first owner. Also, see whether you can get information about the car's maintenance service records. This is a huge gold star if the owner can produce a record of regular maintenance. Does the car have a transferable manufacturer's warranty?

Miles driven are big in determining a car's worth. Generally, average miles are considered to be about 14,000 per year.

Dents and pings are telltale signs that the owner didn't care much. What kind of tread is left on the tires, or do the tires have uneven wear? Each tire is worth at least $100 to replace, not to mention an alignment charge. Push down hard on all four corners of the vehicle. If the car bounces up and down more than three times, the shocks or struts could be bad. Open the hood, and check the oil dipstick. If the oil is very dark or black, that's not a good sign.

If you're still interested enough to test-drive the vehicle, make sure the car engine is cold—in other words, it hasn't been "warmed up." Drive with the windows down somewhere alongside a concrete lane divider or a wall that will bounce any unusual noises back to you. While driving in a safe area, let go of the wheel to see whether the car wants to veer left or right, indicating an alignment problem.

Ask the seller whether you may drive the car to your own mechanic for a quick inspection. No one wants to tie up his or her car, but any confident seller shouldn't object.

Making a Deal

If you can pay a dealer just above the wholesale price but below the retail amount, you've probably done fine. Try for an 8-percent discount off the asking price, and move upward if needed. With a private seller, ask the seller for the absolute bottom line. Also never give more than $100 as good-faith money to hold a vehicle until all the papers are signed, and not a penny more until you see the vehicle's original title with your name on it.

i didn't know that...

WHERE'S THE VIN?

A car's Vehicle Identification Number (**VIN**) can usually be found at the bottom left side of the windshield or on the inside of the driver's door-jamb. Whenever a vehicle is involved in any insurance claim, the car's VIN is recorded in a central data bank. For a fee, online services, such as Carfax.com, will provide you with a car history report, including accidents and insurance claims.

SERVICING— THE BASICS

On the road again...

CHAPTER 13

Let's face it. You expect your car to start, get you where you need to go, and then get you back home. But to keep your car running reliably and safely, there are things you need to know about it and servicing it periodically. For starters, locate your car owner's manual. Keep it in the glove box or someplace handy. Buy an auto-repair manual for your vehicle's year, make, and model. Simple repairs, such as replacing a headlight or what to make of a warning light, are explained.

Engine Fluids—Oil, Antifreeze, Brake and Washer Fluids, More

an early indicator of a problem with oil, antifreeze, or brake fluid is a deposit left by your car wherever you park. Even if you have the car professionally serviced several times a year (every 3,000 to 5,000 miles), it's still a good idea to check these fluids at least once a month or more frequently if you notice spots on your driveway.

Refer to your owner's manual or your repair book for the proper type of oil to use, the correct mixture of antifreeze, and the type of brake fluid to keep on hand. Your manual will also list the correct tire-pressure settings and tell you how often to bring the car back to the dealer or a qualified mechanic for periodic servicing. Having your car serviced entails a thorough inspection under the hood and under the car to check for any damaged or worn parts. The mechanic will also check the brake fluid, spark plugs, and wheel alignment. If the car is still under warranty, take advantage of it.

i didn't know that...

MOTOR OIL WEIGHT
Actually, 10W-30 weight motor oil is universal, but you should refer to your owner's manual for the exact recommendation for your car's engine. The "W" in the 10W-30 indicates the oil's thickness during winter. A cold climate needs a lower weight to keep it from thickening in low temperatures.

HOW TO OPEN THE HOOD

The most difficult part of checking the engine fluids might be simply finding the hood release and safety latch. Yes, releasing and raising your car's hood is usually a two-step process.

It starts with finding the hood release, which is inside the car under the dashboard on the driver's side. After "popping" the hood, you're halfway there. Next, release the safety latch that is located just under the hood in the center. This will allow you to lift the hood and expose the engine. In many cases, there will be a hinged metal rod, which you'll lift and insert into a catch to prop up the hood. Other car hoods, those with a spring or hydraulic pistons, will lift and stay in place.

CHECKING THE ENGINE OIL— MONTHLY

Years ago when a gas station was a service station, an attendant always offered to check your oil and clean your windshield when you stopped to fill the tank. Those days are long gone! But you can easily check the oil yourself—the engine must be off, but it doesn't have to cool down.

You will need to have a rag or paper towel on hand. Then raise the hood, and look for the oil dipstick. (See the top right photo on this page.)

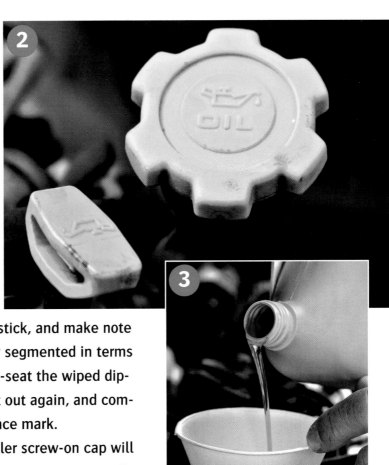

1 Pull out the oil dipstick, and wipe it clean with the rag. Look at the bottom of the stick, and make note of the reference marks, usually segmented in terms of quarts of oil. Reinsert and re-seat the wiped dipstick back in place. Then pull it out again, and compare the oil level to the reference mark.

2 If more oil is needed, the oil filler screw-on cap will be located somewhere on top of the engine. It will have a picture of an oilcan on its face. Unscrew and remove it.

3 Add the oil in full quart amounts using a funnel. Replace the oil cap, and you're done.

Checking the Radiator Coolant—a.k.a. "Antifreeze"

Before you get started, it's important to make sure that the engine is cool. The radiator is in front of the engine in a place where fresh air can rush in and cool off the antifreeze. Never—ever—open a radiator cap when the engine is warm or hot, because engine coolants operate under pressure and you could be badly burned. Do not pour antifreeze directly into the radiator. Instead, follow the black rubber tube (which is connected to the radiator near the cap) to a semiclear plastic reservoir that holds the antifreeze. You can safely open this cap even if the engine is still warm.

Indicator lines on the reservoir container allow you to see the current fluid level and whether more is needed. Usually a 50/50 mix of antifreeze and water will do the trick, but you should consult your owner's manual or call an auto-parts dealer for advice on the exact mixture. It may depend on your climate.

Add the antifreeze using a funnel. Snap the plastic cap back into place, and you're finished. Be sure to clean up any spills because antifreeze tastes sweet to animals and is very harmful if swallowed by pets. If you find the need to routinely add antifreeze, this is a sign that a major problem could be developing and you should have the car checked by a professional—soon.

It's simple to add your own antifreeze. Use a funnel to avoid splatters.

what would you do?

QUICK-LUBE SERVICES

You've decided to use a quick-lube service to grease and oil your car. As you wait, sipping free coffee and watching TV, the service manager calls you out to your car for a conference. You're getting nervous. He shows you all the concerns his technicians have found that should be addressed. This may include replacing your air filter, fuel filter, rear gear fluid, transmission fluid and filter, and rotating your tires. Would you

◀ a. tell them to take care of everything

◀ b. hand them the coupon you cut out of Sunday's paper and get out of there

◀ c. talk to a mechanic you trust about all other maintenance concerns?

The smart answer is "c." Remember, it's the service manager's job to boost revenue—but don't let it be at your expense. In fact, many experts advise not flushing out the transmission fluid in older vehicles, because this could actually cause a transmission problem.

what would you do?

SPRITZ IT

Your car's windshield is so dirty you can barely see out of it, but your wiper-fluid reservoir is empty. Would you

a. fill the reservoir with a household glass cleaner

b. wait for rain, and hope for the best

c. wipe off the window with a glass cleaner, and then go to the store and purchase a gallon of windshield wiper fluid to replenish your supply?

I hope you answered "c." Windshield washer fluid is specially formulated so that it does not freeze in winter, and it cuts through road film and salt. You can find it almost anywhere—even in the supermarket— and it's cheap.

Checking the Brake Fluid

Similar to the antifreeze reservoir, a white, semitransparent reservoir allows you to see the brake-fluid level in most cars today. The brake-fluid reservoir is located on the driver's side under the hood and mounted on the master cylinder. The cap will usually say "DOT." Notice the fill-line marks on the reservoir that indicate whether brake fluid must be added. Consult your owner's manual, or call your local auto-supply dealer to make sure you have the appropriate type of brake fluid for your car. Most likely it will be a DOT3 type.

Keep in mind, low brake fluid is a clear sign that a problem is brewing, and you should make immediate plans to have your brakes checked by a professional.

The process of removing the brake fluid reservoir cap depends on your vehicle. It could involve releasing a bolt, prying off a rubber cap, leveraging a metal tension spring to one side using a screwdriver, or simply unscrewing a plastic cap. Underneath the cap, you might notice two separate reservoir chambers for the front and the rear brakes. The underside of this cap could also have one rubber bladder or two, one for each chamber. This bladder is designed to expand like an accordion to prevent air from filling the void created when brake fluid becomes too low. Air in your brake lines is a bad thing. After filling the reservoir, push the rubber bladder back (flat) into place, and then replace the cap. Once again, if your brake fluid is that low, have your car checked.

Checking the Washer Fluid

You're driving down a wet highway alongside a semitractor trailer, and the road spray from the truck's tires is covering your windshield. You turn on the washer fluid and—you only manage to smear the mud and debris all over the windshield. This is a dangerous situation at 60 miles per hour. It's also a good reason to check your car's washer fluid monthly—or more often if you have to use it frequently.

Locate the washer-fluid reservoir. Again, it's under the hood and in the engine compartment. If your vehicle has a rear window wiper, there will also be a rear washer-fluid reservoir. Unscrew the cap, which will probably be labeled or have an icon on it indicating that it's the washer-fluid reservoir. (Check your owner's manual if you're not sure.) You don't have to be too polite about pouring windshield fluid into the reservoir. I rarely bother with a funnel.

WIPER BLADE REPLACEMENT

Every six to nine months, and particularly after the winter season, you might notice your wiper blades aren't getting the job done. It's not difficult to replace wiper blades. Replacements are sold as inexpensive, rubber refills. You can also purchase the rubber refill and the refill frame as a single, albeit more expensive unit. See your owner's manual for the length you'll need, or on a dry day, bring a wiper with you to match up at the store.

If this is something you'd rather not tackle, drive to a local auto-parts store and ask someone for assistance. An employee will most likely come out from behind the counter, pick out the correct replacements, and install the new blades, all within five minutes. If he refuses a tip, bring in some coffee and donuts for the staff the next morning. It's a small investment, and they will remember you.

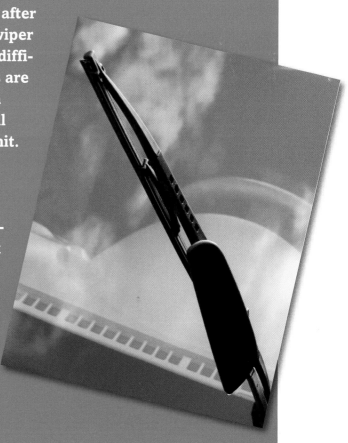

The Lights and Other Electrical Matters

just as in your home, lightbulbs will burn out in your car. And just like your home, your car also has a fuse box. Taillights burn out more often than headlights, but it's unlikely that both the left and right sides will burn out at the same time.

Checking all the lights is an easy process, but one that is often ignored or forgotten—until a police officer pulls you over and hands you a ticket. So check your car's lights monthly. Once the sun goes down, start the ignition; turn on the headlights; and walk around the car. Turn on the high beams; and look again at the front headlights. Don't forget to check both the left and right turn signals, too.

Most taillights have a dual filament. One operates when the lights are on, and the other kicks in with a brighter glow when the brakes are applied or when you are signaling to turn. Usually, if the turn signals work, so too will the brake lights, but it is best to check. If you're on your own, simply back in the car so that you can see the brake-light reflection against the garage wall. That's it, and it takes two minutes tops.

A burned-out bulb can prevent the turn signal from working. But if both the right and left turn signals do not work, there's a good chance your car has a bad

"flasher," which is
usually located at or near the fuse
box. If both the right and left taillights and both
brake lights do not work at all, the problem is most likely as simple
as a blown fuse.

Changing a bulb, signal flasher, or fuse is not difficult, and it's a
quick, inexpensive do-it-yourself fix. Usually the trick is isolating and
gaining access to the problem. Sometimes just finding the location of
the fuse panel is a tough chore, and so is figuring out whether you can
reach the taillight bulbs from inside the trunk. Most often you can get
to the taillight bulbs by using a screwdriver, peeling back some trunk
carpeting, or a combination of both. This is when the owner or repair
manual will save you time.

Replacement bulbs and fuses can be picked up in the automotive
section of many major retail stores. Once again, you might try appealing to the local auto-parts-store guy mentioned earlier for some help.

**For safety's sake,
make sure your car's
head- and tail-lights
are working. Check
the brake lights,
routinely, too.**

The Car Battery

Today, most car batteries are maintenance-free, although some might have a green-eye check device. This cell window on top of the battery provides a green glow indicating that the battery is good—in theory. However, this green glow actually may mean that one part of the battery cell is good, but not necessarily the entire thing. Pay more attention to your car battery's age than the green glow of envy.

Most car batteries are designed to last between 36 to 48 months. Listen for the warning signs of a struggle your car may be having turning over the engine. If your car's battery is nearing the end of its design life, don't wait for it to fail—replace it because it will likely fail the day after its design-life date.

Cold weather will diminish a car battery's capability. If you live in a cold climate, consider a battery's "cold cranking amps" (or CCA). Cranking amps indicate a battery's strength at 32 degrees Fahrenheit. A battery's cold cranking amps is its strength at 0 degrees Fahrenheit. A battery needs a minimum 10.5 amps to keep a car running. Check your manual for the recommended CCA rating for your vehicle's battery.

JUMP-STARTING A DEAD BATTERY

In freezing weather, if your battery seems to have died—the ignition won't turn over and the lights and radio don't work—try this: turn on your headlights for 10 seconds; shut them off; and then try starting the ignition. This is referred to as "waking up the battery." If that doesn't work, you may be able to solve your problem by jump-starting the car. Basically, this means getting a charge from another vehicle. You'll need jumper cables, and this is why it's a good idea to keep a set in your car. If you don't have them, see whether someone nearby has a set you can use.

But first, make sure your owner's manual indicates that jump-starting will not damage your vehicle. If it's not contraindicated in your owner's manual, proceed. Here's how.

1 Make sure both vehicles are facing each other, very close, without touching. Switch off the ignition on both of the cars.

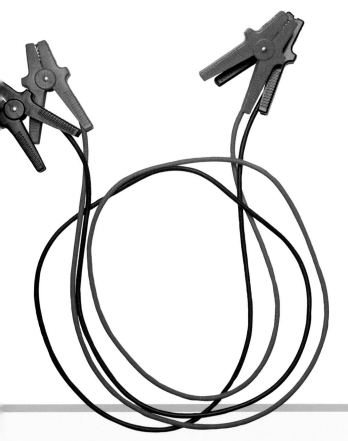

i didn't know that...

CRANKING?

The term "cranking amps" comes from the old days of automobiles when the engines had to be manually cranked, or turned over, by hand. Then one day, someone invented the automatic starter, which lets the car's battery do all the work of turning over the engine to start it.

2 Attach the jaw of the red jumper cable to the "+" or the positive ("POS") battery terminal on both vehicles. Be careful not to touch any metal surface other than the battery.

Attach the jaws of the black jumper cable to the "−" or the negative ("NEG") terminal of the working battery.

To complete the circuit, attach the other end of the black cable a few feet away from the dead battery, finding a spot on the metal chassis (frame) or the metal engine block— but not to any electrical component.

Start the engine of the car that has the working battery. Apply the gas slightly to rev the engine just a bit. Then start the car with the dead battery.

3 With both cars running, remove the cables in the reverse order of how you attached them. Don't let them touch until you have removed them from both batteries.

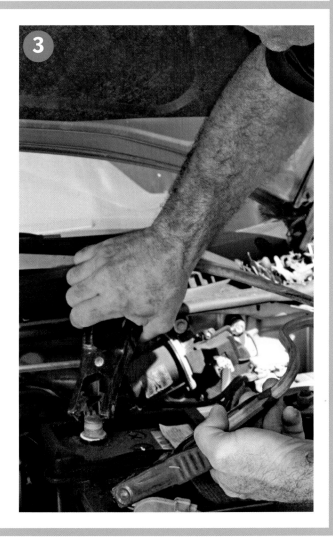

GETTING AROUND SAFELY

There are situations that can either compromise your safety on the road or, at the very least, cause you stress. No one likes to get pulled over by the police, but if it happens to you, there's a way to handle the situation that will keep it from escalating into something more than a simple traffic violation. You should also know what you are expected to do—and what you should do—in case you are in a car accident.

Getting Pulled Over by the Police

olice officers are killed more often in routine traffic stops than in any other police situation. You may be nervous, aggravated, or upset—but get over it quickly. A police officer never knows what to expect when he or she approaches a stopped vehicle. They deserve your respect.

Always pull over to the far right lane unless instructed otherwise by the officer, and turn on your emergency flashers. Immediately roll down your window just enough to speak through it, shut off the radio, and if you're smoking, put the cigarette in the ashtray. If you're stopped at night, turn on your interior light so the officer can see inside the car.

Stay in your car unless you're told to get out of it, place both hands on the steering wheel, and wait for instructions. Don't start rummaging for your wallet, license, or registration until the officer asks for them and can clearly see what you are doing. For all he knows, you could be reaching for a gun.

what would you do?

YOU'RE RIGHT TO BE CONCERNED

You are signaled to pull over in a remote or poorly lit location by an unmarked police car or an officer not in uniform. Would you

◀ a. pull over, keep the engine running and the doors locked, and slightly lower the window

◀ b. just keep going

◀ c. pull over, get out of your car, and wait for the officer to approach you?

The answer is "a." Do not turn off the engine or get out of the car. If the officer asks you to do so, explain your concerns and request a second officer to the scene, or ask the officer to hold onto your driver's license as he follows you to a less remote area. A good officer should be understanding and cooperative. If he's not, that's a red flag. Stay in your car; call 911 from your cell phone to report the situation; and wait. As a last resort, drive away slowly with your flashers on to a safer, more populated location. You can always deal with the consequences later. Ultimately, this is your call and your safety.

Never leave the scene of a accident. Notify the police, and try to remain calm while you wait for them.

If You're Involved in a Car Accident

Call the police immediately. Let them know whether there are injuries, and wait for the police to arrive. Unless the damage is minimal, do not move your vehicle until instructed to do so by the police. Regardless of how minor the collision, file a police report or Bureau of Motor Vehicles (BMV) Crash Report, and notify your insurance company within 24 hours. On the report, keep the wording brief and accurate, but don't write anything that implies that you are at fault.

If you feel you are injured, stay in the vehicle until help arrives. Make no statements as to your physical condition unless asked by the police or paramedics. After the incident, make a visit to the emergency room and obtain a medical report.

After any collision, never leave the scene without exchanging information with the other driver. Exchange as much information about the crash as possible, the more the better. This is why you should keep a pen and, ideally, a disposable camera in your glove box. A picture really is worth a thousand words.

Be wary if the other driver tries to convince you that because there is no "real damage" there is no need to file a police report. Don't be persuaded by the other driver's offer of money to cover the damages, either. The next thing you know, he or she may file a report with your license-plate number claiming you left the scene after the accident, and he or she may produce "witnesses."

INFORMATION TO REQUEST

Collect the following information on the other car:

• driver's name, address, and phone number

• description of the other car—its make, color, and model

• license-plate number

• date, time of day, and road conditions

• police officer's name and badge number

• witnesses —if any

And if possible:

• driver's license number, if offered

• car registration information

• insured's name, address, and phone number (if different from the driver's)

• insurance policy number

Winter Driving

ideally, you will begin thinking about winter driving and safety when you pick out your new car. A sporty little roadster looks great for nine months of the year, but if it can't get you where you need to go safely the rest of the time, maybe you need a different car. Severe winter-weather driving is all about planning, resistance, traction, and momentum. Bridges, overpasses, and ramps all freeze long before ground-level roads and highways, so be particularly careful once the warm-weather season ends.

Planning and Resistance

When trees have shed their leaves, put a small shovel in the trunk and a scraper brush in the back seat, and start adding a pint of gas-line antifreeze to the tank every other time you fill up. Gas tanks develop condensation, and gas-line antifreeze helps keep the water from freezing and plugging the gas lines.

Before the snow sets in, think about alternative routes. Look for the path of least resistance. Rule out hilly shortcuts or back roads that won't be salted or plowed until well after a storm. Snow delivers resistance to your car's tires. Thinner tires actually encounter less resistance than those that are wider. If you become stuck, make sure your front tires are pointed perfectly straight. A straight tire offers less resistance than one that is angled for a turn.

Traction and Momentum

Front-wheel drive cars have the weight of the engine directly over the drive wheels, greatly enhancing traction and pulling the car through the snow. On the other hand, a lightweight rear-wheel drive car not only lacks weight over the drive wheels but must also push the heavier front of the car through the snow. This can be a real problem, particularly on an incline.

If you have a rear-wheel drive car, keep the gas tank full and pick up two or three 80-pound sandbags (or the equivalent), and place them in the trunk. Sandbags can be purchased at any home-improvement center. The added weight helps the rear wheels dig into the snow. Even if you have a front-wheel drive car, pick up a bag. Sand is very

helpful if you become stuck. Throw handfuls of sand directly under, and several feet in front of, both drive wheels.

Objects in motion tend to stay in motion. That's Newton's first law of motion, the Law of Inertia. It takes a great deal of force to move your car forward from a dead stop. In snow, the objective is to keep your car moving forward—no matter how slowly—and to avoid stopping if possible. This is particularly true when approaching a traffic light at the top of an incline. Slow down, and try to time the light, keeping your car moving forward. However, if you get stuck on an incline, either break out the sand or plan on backing the car down the hill. Your best option? Avoid the hill!

what would you do?

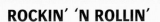

ROCKIN' 'N ROLLIN'

Your car is stuck, and your drive tires have created a rut. You can't get your car out of it. Would you

◀ a. put the petal to the medal
◀ b. rock the car back and forth
◀ c. call a tow truck?

The correct answer is "b." Think back to when you were a kid on a swing and how the repetitive pendulum-like action caused you to go faster and higher with each swing. It takes technique, but you want to create this same type of rocking motion with the vehicle. Rapidly alternating the forward and reverse gears while at the same time applying and letting off the accelerator pedal creates the back-and-forth rocking motion needed to get out of the rut. If the car stops rocking, you're not alternating fast enough. Again, make sure your front wheels are perfectly straight, not turned.

ABOUT YOUR

part III

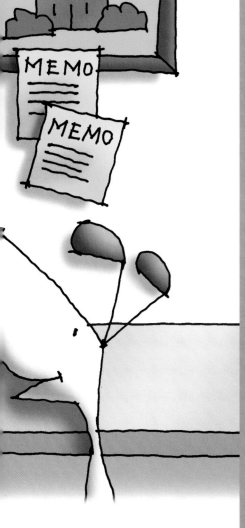

CAREER

Today's job market is tough. If you're applying for a job, make the best impression possible, starting with a strong résumé. Most personnel screeners see hundreds of them. How can you keep yours from winding up in the paper shreader? Include a cover letter that is unique and engaging, rather than a general mass mailer. And however you submit your resume, over email, fax, or snail mail, check your spelling. Errors will definitely win yours a place in the reject pile.

A Good Impression

be concise. No one wants to read a résumé that is more than two pages long. It you can keep it to one page, all the better. As for the order in which to present information about yourself, start with your strong suit. If that is your job experience, list it first. If it's your education, begin with your school and college history. (Don't list the year of graduation, which is an age qualifier.) Be fair to yourself, but don't embellish your skills and strengths.

Prepare a list of personal references to take with you, and have it ready to produce if asked for at an interview. Make sure everyone on that list is aware that they may receive a call from a prospective employer asking about you.

Interviewing for a Job

On a first interview, the company is interested in your interpersonal skills and whether you would fit into the organization. Appearance is part of it. Dress for success—this is not the time or place for bling or cowboy-hat individuality.

Begin each meeting with a smile, a firm handshake, and direct eye contact with your interviewer. Make eye contact throughout the interview; this suggests self-confidence and sincerity. When asked a question, a candidate who turns away, looks into the air, or looks down at his or her shoes suggests weakness and doubt to the interviewer. Don't offer aimless, meandering answers to questions or try to bloat your skills, either. These are all turnoffs. Avoid statements such as, "I'm thinking about doing such-and-such to better myself." That's a confession that you have weaknesses. Never speak poorly of any previous employer no matter how bad the experience. That's a big red flag.

Keep in mind that few people are hired after the first interview. If you are doing well in the process, expect a second or even a third interview before a job offer is made. A day or so after an interview, mail a brief but cordial note to each person you met, thanking them for their time and reaffirming your interest in the position. Don't be overly effusive.

QUESTIONS

Here are some basic questions you should be prepared to field during a job interview. Have specific examples to support your answers. I'll never forget a candidate who described his top strength as "communication" but could not explain why!

1. **What do you already know about the company?** This reveals your initiative and interest.
2. **What top five strengths would you bring to this position?** This indicates your confidence in your abilities.
3. **Why do you believe that you possess these strengths?** If you can't give examples, you're probably making up stuff—and the interviewer will know it.
4. **What did you like most about your last position?**

YOU SHOULD ANTICIPATE

Your answer will reveal more about your previous job responsibilities.

5. What would you say was your greatest accomplishment at your last job?

   This is another way of indicating your initiative.

6. Why do you wish to leave your current job?

   The interviewer might really be saying, "Give me some dirt." Don't do it.

7. How do you approach the workday?

   Are you a planner or a to-do-list type, or do you run by the seat of your pants?

8. Can you describe a typical day at your last job?

   This reveals whether you are strictly a 9-to-5 person or someone who lets the workload define your hours.

9. How would you react to an assignment that is handed to you at the end of the day?

   The interviewer wants to know how much of a commitment you are willing to make.

10. What skills would you like to improve?

    Your answer shows whether you are serious about achieving your full potential.

11. How would you handle a problem employee?

    This indicates whether you can communicate and connect with other people.

12. Would you prefer to use a meeting, phone call, or email to resolve a problem?

    Again, your answer reveals your "people skills."

13. What issues would concern you about working in a group or team atmosphere?

    Is self-recognition or team results more important to you?

14. Are you willing to travel or relocate?

    If this is an issue, say so now.

15. What questions do you have about the job or this company?

    Make sure you have prepared at least two for each interviewer. There's nothing more deflating than a candidate who shakes his or her head, and says, "I don't have any questions." How could you not have questions? You want to work there, right?

Powerful Words for a Winning Resume

Accelerated
Accomplished
Achieved
Adapted
Advised
Administered
Analyzed
Approved
Arranged
Assembled
Budgeted
Built
Calculated
Completed
Formulated
Founded

Conceived
Conducted
Coordinate͏
Cre͏
Del͏
Deli͏
Dem͏
Deve͏
Devis͏
Direc͏
Edited͏
Establ͏
Estima
Evalua͏
Expand
Motivat͏

Generated
Implemented

Operated
Organ͏

RESUME

CAREER SUMMARY

18 years in civil design and co͏
structural designer in consulti͏
mmercial building and cemer͏
industry thru. Currently a͏
roject Greenfield Ar͏

I, AISC, ASC
NS
Familia͏
NEMA St͏

WORK EXPERIENCE

June 2001 – Present   Civil Engineer II

Has been involved
international and local

Traveling for Business

given all the hassles of flight schedules, if the distance is less than a three-hour drive, going by car might be a good idea. This is particularly true if you would be renting a car at your destination anyway. Rent the car locally; drive to your destination; and return the car once you're home. Of course, when you travel a distance for business, it's typically by plane.

If you don't already have one, get a passport. In these days of "homeland security," a passport is required for traveling anywhere outside of the United States, and that includes Canada, Mexico, Bermuda, and the Caribbean region. It's also an excellent form of identification, which you can use to board a plane or rent a car. Due to the time involved in processing a passport, don't wait until you need one. Go online or visit your local post office for details and an application. In a pinch, you can have a passport expedited, but it's expensive.

Use a separate credit card, in particular one that is airline-sponsored, for business expenses only. Join frequent-flyer programs with all of the major airlines, frequent-stay programs with all major hotel chains, and pre-ferred-customer programs with all the major rental-car companies.

Your travel profile should include your cell phone number as the primary contact number to call in the event of a flight change or cancellation. Frequent travelers I know also prefer using one-stop-shopper online travel companies to book reservations for flights, hotels, and rental cars.

TRAVEL TIPS

- If you're leaving your car in the airport's long-term parking lot, remove anything that contains your home address.
- If you label a bag "fragile," it will be loaded on the plane so that it comes out of the baggage carousel first.
- If you're traveling overseas, get the generic name of your prescriptions; brand names differ.
- Never take a hotel room that's on the first floor or one that is near an elevator or ice machine.
- If you're traveling internationally, get a converter and an outlet adapter for electrical appliances, such as your blow dryer.
- Make a photocopy of your passport, and keep that in a different place from your passport.
- Overseas, use your ATM card at a bank. It is the lowest-cost source for local currency and for getting the best exchange rate.

Flight, Hotel, and Rental-Car Advice

Creating a frequent-flyer account and profile with airlines not only accumulates mileage points but also makes you eligible for free seating upgrades when they are available. A frequent-stay account with a major hotel chain helps to increase air-travel points and allows you to specify floor and room preferences.

A "preferred customer" loyalty program with a rental-car company also adds to your air-travel points and saves you time. Rather than dragging your luggage to the rental counter and waiting in line, you can be dropped off at your preselected waiting vehicle. You can waive the extended rental-vehicle insurance coverage if you're covered by a corporate insurance policy.

Book a flight as far in advance as possible in order to get a good price and seat selection. When you are traveling internationally, getting through customs can sometimes be a four- to six-hour ordeal. Keep this in mind when planning any connecting flights. If the booking is within 90 minutes, the first airline will not take responsibility for the missed connection. However, if you allow at least two hours between the landing and departure time of the two planes, the first airline will be obligated to reimburse you for your missed connection.

i didn't know that...

GETTING FROM GATE TO GATE

Whenever you book a flight that requires changing planes, familiarize yourself with the airport and departure gates. They may be at opposite ends of the airport, meaning you may have to scramble to get to your connecting flight on time. Most major airport maps can be found online. Use them, and plan accordingly.

IT'S YOUR MONEY; YOU EARNED IT

The average life expectancy for a woman is 90; for a man, it's 80. The average retirement age is 62. This means a woman will need about 28 years of post-retirement financial support; a man will need about 18 years. Two-thirds of women over age 65 have no pension other than Social Security payments, which are based on your highest 35 years of earnings. (Each year you didn't work is added in as $0, significantly lowering your monthly benefit.) Think about it.

Savings and Investments

in 1943, the government passed a law making sure you paid your taxes first by withholding them from your paycheck. You should save in the same way, by paying yourself second. Set up direct deposit for your paycheck, and try to put aside 15 percent of your pay.

Think of it this way: time is money. For example, Mary and Carol are the same age. Mary has saved $25 per week from the time she was 25 years old. Carol, at age 45, starts saving the same amount each month. Both earn 8 percent interest on their money. When they each reach age 65, Carol's $24,000 investment will have grown to $57,000 while Mary's $48,000 investment will have grown to $324,000. Why? It's the power of compounding interest. Compounding interest is interest earning interest on the interest. Do it.

EARNED INTEREST

◀ At an annual 4 percent interest return, you double your money in 18 years.

◀ At 8 percent, you double your money in 9 years.

◀ At 10 percent, you double your money in 7.5 years.

◀ At 15 percent, you double your money in 5 years.

PAYING WITH PLASTIC— CREDIT CARDS

A credit card is a license to borrow the bank's money that costs the average family over $1,000 per year in interest payments. If you save and invest $1,000 instead, after 20 years you will have accrued close to $50,000—just for refusing the bank's money to buy things you'll have to pay for anyway.

Never pay credit-card finance charges. Pay off the entire balance each month with money from your checking account. If you don't have it, don't spend it.

By the way, banks pay you only 2 percent interest on the money you lend them (savings), but charge you up to 20 to 30 percent on money they lend you via credit cards. Can you imagine the lines if a grocery store offered a 20-percent discount if you paid in cash?

Debit cards are great for limiting your exposure; however, your purchases are not protected by your bank. If you dispute a charge or wish to return a purchase or feel a service did not meet your expectation, your bank will immediately cancel the charge, but if that same purchase were made with a debit card, you would probably be out of luck.

Employer Retirement Programs

i f a rich uncle said to you, "Promise me not to spend the money until you retire, and I'll match $17 out of my own pocket for every $25 per week you save," would you be interested? This scenario is similar to a common 401K, 403B, or 457B retirement plan, where your employer matches $1 for each $1 you save up to the first 2 percent of your salary, and then an additional $.50 per $1 you save up to the next 3 percent of your salary. With nontaxable compounding interest, at the end of 30 years your $39,000 personal contribution could accumulate to $154,000!

How much money should you have in order to comfortably retire? Some experts say you need half the annual income in retirement that you had while you were working. But this depends on many unpredictable factors, including but not limited to healthcare, inflation, whether the government will continue Social Security or another plan for senior care, and your lifestyle. Again, save, save, save.

MONEY TIPS

- Invest in real estate. Seventy percent of all millionaires in the U.S. have made their fortunes in real estate.
- Live below your means. Spend at a level of one or two pay increases behind what you currently earn, and invest the difference.
- A home meal is a half hour's pay. A meal at a nice restaurant is a half-day's pay.
- Drop the health-club membership and cable-TV package you rarely use.
- Don't use money saved on bargains for purchases you were not planning to make.
- At the beginning of each new sales week, carefully watch the cashier's screen as your groceries are scanned.
- If you own a cell phone, based on the features of the plan (nights, weekends, long distance), consider canceling your landline service altogether.
- If you don't use your cell phone often, drop that plan and buy a prepaid calling card or a prepaid cell phone instead.
- Refinance your mortgage when interest rates are low, but be mindful of the extra closing costs and the length of the term.
- Call your credit-card bank, and simply ask for a better Annual Percentage Rate financing rate (APR).
- If you're paying monthly credit-card finance charges, get rid of the card.
- Don't include tax when factoring tips. Make sure a tip hasn't already been added to the bill, which often happens when dining with large groups.

Taxes, Taxes, and More Taxes...

ncome tax, property tax, Social Security tax, gasoline tax, meal tax, sales tax, excise tax, capital-gains tax—believe it or not, taxes will be among the biggest expenses in your life.

Your earnings less deductions equals your taxable income. Your taxable income is multiplied by a sliding tax rate to determine what you owe the government. The higher your taxable income, the higher your tax rate will be.

One way to lower your taxes is by decreasing your earned income—not quite as bad as it sounds. Having pretax income set aside into an employer's flexible medical spending account or retirement plan allows you to divert some of your taxable earnings.

The pretaxed money you have accumulated in a 401K, 403B, or an IRA is taxed when you take out the money (disbursements) when you retire, when your income-tax rate should be much lower. A Roth IRA is funded with after-tax money (take-home pay), and this will not be taxed again when you take the money out at retirement.

Taxes can also be reduced by direct tax credits. The final tax you owe is matched against the taxes you have paid or had your employer withhold throughout the year. To square up, you either write a check to the Internal Revenue Service or receive a refund from the federal government.

You must file a tax return no later than April 15 each year regardless of whether you are owed a refund or not. Keep in mind, a tax refund doesn't always mean you paid no taxes. More likely, it means you paid more than you should have, and you provided the government an interest-free loan all year out of your own pocket.

Pick up a tax-preparation software program. These programs walk you step by step through the complication that is the U.S. tax code and could save you $150 to $300 each year in tax-preparation fees from a Certified Public Accountant (CPA).

i didn't know that...

EARNED INTEREST

Remember Mary from the earlier example? Let's say she retires at age 65. While she may have stopped working, her money did not. Assuming her money continues to earn 8 percent on her $324,000, and she withdraws only the interest, she would have close to $26,000 of taxable interest income each year, not to mention her Social Security retirement benefit.

This might sound appealing when thinking in today's dollars, but after 20 years of an average inflation rate at 3.5 percent per year, $26,000 will only buy $13,000 worth of goods or services. Ask your parents what they paid for their first home or first car.

If you start at age 22 and can save 15 percent of your gross income (income before deductions, credits, and taxes) each year, with a sound investment plan you should be able to retain the same lifestyle in retirement as you had in your working years. Search out a professional financial advisor and stay with the plan.

INDEX

credits

All illustrations by Tad Herr.

Note: DT=Dreamstime.com

Front Cover: *left* Tony Giammarino/Giammarino & Dworkin; *center* Vladimir Daragan/DT; *right* Yuri Arcurs/DT **Back Cover:** *top* Creativefire/DT; *middle* 350jb/DT; *bottom* Hongqi Zhang/DT **page 2:** *top* Hieng Ling Tie/DT; *center* Steve Husk/DT; *bottom* Gunnar3000/DT **page 8:** Svand/DT **pages 12–13:** courtesy of IKEA **pages 14–15:** Volodymyr Kyrylyuk/DT **page 16:** Nilanjan Bhattacharya/DT **page 17:** Ron Chapple Studios/DT **pages 18–19:** Nilanjan Bhattacharya/DT **pages 20–21:** Hieng Ling Tie/DT **pages 22–23:** Olivier Le Queinec/DT **page 26:** Yukchong Kwan/DT **page 27:** Paulpaladin/DT **pages 28–31:** Olivier Le Queinec/DT **page 32:** *top* Lisa Turay/DT; *bottom* Starletdarlene/DT **page 33:** Tony Giammarino/Giammarino & Dworkin, design: Cheryl Palmore **pages 34–35:** Aoldman/DT **pages 36–37:** Scubabartek/DT **page 39:** Picstudio/DT (pliers); Hot99/DT (screwdriver); Ron Chapple Studios/DT (drill); Jose Manuel Gelpi Diaz/DT (ladder); Fibobjects/DT (measuring tape) **page 41:** Elisabeth Coelfen/DT **pages 42–43:** Anne Gummerson **page 44:** Gualberto Becerra/DT **page 45:** Martin Green/DT **page 46:** Creativefire/DT **page 48:** John Parsekian/CH **page 49:** Alistair Cotton/DT **page 50:** courtesy of York Wallcoverings **pages 52–53:** John Parsekian/CH **pages 54–55:** Anne Gummerson **pages 56–57:** Catherine Lall/DT **page 58:** *top* Freeze Frame Studio/CH; *bottom* Brian C. Nieves/CH **page 60:** *left* Brian C. Nieves/CH; *right* John Parsekian/CH **pages 61–65:** Brian C. Nieves/CH **pages 66–67:** courtesy of Moen **pages 68–69:** John Parsekian/CH **pages 71–75:** Merle Henkenius/CH **pages 76–77:** Starletdarlene/DT **pages 78–79:** *left* Nancy Dressel/DT; *right* Knightshade/DT **page 80:** Merle Henkenius/CH **pages 81–82:** courtesy of Whirlpool **page 85:** courtesy of Kenmore, Whirlpool Corp. **page 86:** courtesy of Maytag, Whirlpool Corp. **page 88:** John Parsekian/CH **page 89:** Brian C. Nieves/CH **pages 90–91:** courtesy of KitchenAid, Whirlpool Corp. **pages 92–93:** courtesy of Moen **page 95:** Natalia Bratslavsky/DT **page 97:** courtesy of Vermont Castings **pages 98–99:** Olson Photographic, LLC **page 100:** Jack Schiffer/DT **page 101:** John Parsekian/CH **page 102:** Cynthia Farmer/DT **pages 104–105:** courtesy of CertainTeed **pages 106–107:** *top center* courtesy of MonierLifetile LLC; *bottom center* Lastdays1/DT; *right* courtesy of DaVinci Roofscapes **page 108:** Orange Line Media/DT **page 109:** Mark Hryciw/DT **page 110:** John Parsekian/CH **page 111:** courtesy of EDCO **page 112:** Elena Elisseeva/DT **page 113:** Crystal Craig/DT **page 114:** Kenneth Sponsler/DT **pages 118–119:** Mike Brake/DT **page 120:** Steve Husk/DT **page 123:** Snaprender/DT **page 124:** Raynald Bélanger/DT **pages 126–127:** Susan Leggett/DT **page 129:** *top* Vladimir Mucibabic/DT; *center* Photographer/DT; *bottom* Susy56/DT **pages 130–131:** Brian Humek/DT **page 132:** Robert Byron/DT **page 133:** *top* 350jb/DT; *bottom* Paradoks_blizanaca/DT **page 134:** *top* Linqong/DT; *bottom* Tt/DT **page 135:** Ian Francis/DT **page 136:** *left* Tracy Jibbens/DT; *right* Jennifer Thompson/DT **page 137:** *top* Jon Helgason/DT; *bottom right* Lisa F. Young/DT; *bottom left* Jennifer Thompson/DT **pages 138–139:** Snehitdesign/DT **page 140:** Lisa F. Young/DT **page 141:** Robert Mizerek/DT **page 142:** Robert Pernell/DT **page 143:** Lastdays1/DT **page 144:** Taavi Toomasson/DT **page 145:** Intst/DT **pages 148–149:** Iqoncept/DT **page 151:** Ragsac19/DT **page 152:** Juriah Mosin/DT **pages 154–155:** Vinicius Tupinamba/DT

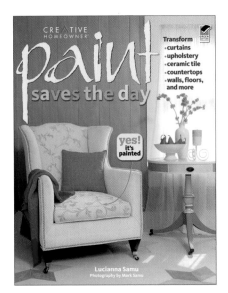
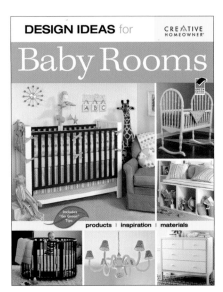
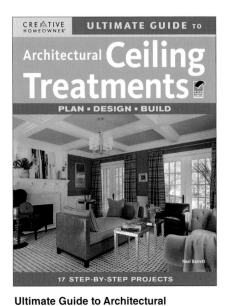
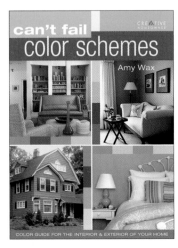
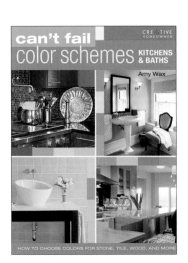
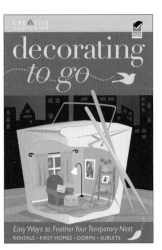